A Star Mastering

The Feminine Enigma

Duchess Nivin ElGamal of Lamberton

A Star Mastering - The Feminine Enigma
by Duchess Nivin ElGamal of Lamberton

To everyone who feels that The Feminine Enigma speaks directly to them—you're absolutely right. And to those who feel the gratitude within these pages is meant for them—you're right as well. My heartfelt thanks go out to each of you.

This book is dedicated to the beautiful, strong, independent, ambitious, joyful, spontaneous, and inquisitive woman.

A special thank you to everyone who shared their experiences and stories with me, honoring their privacy along the way.

Acknowledgements

Special thanks to everyone who knows their own worth.

Copyright Information

ISBN: 9781917601511

duchessoflamberton@gmail.com

Contents

Introduction

Have you ever asked yourself, "What is the most important thing to me after health and my basic needs in life?" If so, you're not alone. The most common question we receive is about men and your relationships with them. Where does the issue lie? Men have often been viewed as pillars of strength and confidence, while women are perceived as subordinate, caught in a demand-supply imbalance that feels unjust.

The Feminine Enigma represents the voices of passionate women — especially women in countries dominated by men — who are skilled in the arts of life, love, and relationships. Yet, it also brings to life the mindset of men, creating a blend of masculine logic and emotion.

Why do so many women dedicate themselves to men burdened by insecurities and inner conflicts, offering undying loyalty only to find heartache? Why choose a path of self-sacrifice, loving someone distant—often in another world, figuratively or literally? Instead, consider the value of a partner who truly respects family and shares meaningful values and principles. You deserve a partner who sees you as irreplaceable, not someone who belittles you or your children.

In this book, you'll discover how to pursue a partnership of integrity and avoid relationships that don't honor your worth. Learn to cherish yourself and recognize what you genuinely deserve in a relationship. A woman's presence is essential because she intuitively understands emotions in a way that men often do not. Men tend to conceal their vulnerabilities, rarely revealing what they truly value in a woman. Yet every man seeks a woman who understands him, challenges him, and brings a sense of peace and tenderness into his life. Beneath this desire lies something deeply personal, something men rarely disclose.

As women, we have an extraordinary ability to read emotions, and through experience, we learn to interpret a man's unspoken feelings, even when he tries to shield them. It's often in these unguarded moments that a man's inner thoughts become visible to us, allowing us to see his true self.

Perhaps you're wondering, "Why do I attract men who don't want to commit? Who is the woman who captures his heart? How does she spark a love that lasts?" This book will answer these questions and more.

Just as you might follow a diet for physical well-being, there is an emotional 'diet'—one that cleanses your mind from misplaced love, excessive giving, and vulnerability that isn't reciprocated. This 'diet' nurtures your soul with wisdom, self-respect, and happiness.

The Feminine Enigma dives into the complexities of love and self-worth. In exploring concepts like the "Devil's Daughter," we look at the unique balance some women achieve, blending femininity, beauty, calmness, and logic to connect with men in a profound way. This book encourages even a small change in society's perception and aims to inspire self-love and personal growth.

As the British poet John Keats once reflected, "A thing of beauty is a joy forever…." With The Feminine Enigma, we present a fresh perspective, offering insights not only into the feminine heart but also into the male psyche. Most men say, "I read more than a book about femininity word by word… And I still don't know what goes on in women's minds." With The Feminine Enigma, we present a fresh perspective, offering insights not only into the feminine heart but also into the male psyche.

For personal consultations, reach out on Instagram @duchess_nivin_elgamal_official or request a phone call.

Chapter 1

The Eternal Journey of Soulmates

As we draw to the close of this exploration of soulmates, it is evident that the concept transcends cultures, religions, and time itself. From ancient wisdom traditions to modern love stories, the idea of a soulmate captures our imagination and speaks to our deepest longing for connection. It is more than just a romantic notion; it is a spiritual truth, reflected in the many paths of faith and human experience.

Soulmates in Different Religious Traditions

The idea of soulmates, though articulated differently, is present in almost every major religion. Each tradition offers its own unique perspective on the nature of soul connections, yet all share a common thread: the belief that certain relationships are destined, powerful, and transcendent.

1. Hinduism: The Eternal Union of Souls

In Hinduism, the concept of a soulmate is often intertwined with the idea of karma and reincarnation. The belief is that souls are bound together by their karmic ties, and these connections can span lifetimes. This is seen in the story of

Radha and Krishna, one of the most revered and celebrated couples in Hindu mythology. Their love is considered divine, transcending the physical realm. Radha is seen as Krishna's eternal consort, representing the soul's deep longing for unity with the divine.

Hindu texts also speak of "***Ardhanarishvara***," the androgynous form of the god Shiva, which symbolizes the union of the masculine and feminine energies. This depiction suggests that soulmates are not just romantic partners but also spiritual counterparts, completing and balancing each other.

Real-life Example: "***Ram and Sita***"
The story of Ram and Sita from the Ramayana is a powerful example of soulmate connections in Hinduism. Despite enduring separation, trials, and tribulations, their love remained steadfast. Ram and Sita are often invoked as the ideal couple, embodying the virtues of loyalty, commitment, and divine love.

2. Christianity: A Covenant of Souls

In Christianity, the idea of soulmates is closely linked to the sacrament of marriage. Many Christian denominations believe that marriage is a covenant, a sacred bond established by God. This bond reflects the relationship between Christ and the Church, emphasizing unity, love, and self-sacrifice. The concept of "one flesh" mentioned in the Bible (Genesis 2:24) suggests that in marriage, two souls are united in a profound and spiritual way.

Some Christians believe that God has a specific person in mind for each individual, a "divinely ordained" soulmate. This belief is rooted in the idea that God is sovereign and knows the deepest desires of our hearts. However, others hold that while God guides us, we have the free will to choose our partner, and any marriage entered into with love and commitment can become a sacred union.

Real-life Example: "**C.S. Lewis and Joy Davidman**"
The love story of C.S. Lewis, the renowned Christian author, and Joy Davidman is often cited as an example of a deep soulmate connection. Both had suffered significant personal losses before they met. Their love, though brief due to Joy's untimely death, was profound and transformative for Lewis, who wrote about their relationship in his book "A Grief Observed." Their bond was one of intellectual, emotional, and spiritual depth.

3. **Islam: A Divine Partnership**

In Islam, marriage is seen as a sign of God's mercy and a means of achieving spiritual completeness. The Qur'an describes marriage as a "sign" of God's creation, emphasizing that spouses are garments for one another, providing mutual comfort, protection, and support (Qur'an 30:21). This idea aligns with the concept of soulmates, where two people are destined to complement and support each other in their journey toward spiritual fulfillment.
The Islamic tradition also holds that souls were created in pairs, and these pairs are destined to find each other in this life or the next. This belief is encapsulated in the idea of

"***qadar***" or divine decree, suggesting that certain relationships are written by God long before we are born.

Real-life Example: "**Prophet Muhammad and Khadijah**" The relationship between Prophet Muhammad and his first wife, Khadijah, is often held as an ideal example of a spiritual and loving partnership in Islam. Khadijah was not only his wife but also his closest confidant, supporter, and friend.

Their relationship was built on mutual respect, trust, and love, which lasted until her death. Even after her passing, the Prophet Muhammad spoke of her with great reverence and affection, reflecting the deep soulmate connection they shared.

4. **Judaism: Bashert – The Predestined One**

In Jewish tradition, the concept of a soulmate is known as "bashert," which means destiny or predestination. The Talmud teaches that forty days before a child is born, a voice from heaven announces who that child's soulmate will be. This belief underscores the idea that certain relationships are divinely ordained.

Judaism also emphasizes the importance of partnership in marriage. The Kabbalistic tradition speaks of the "tikkun" or spiritual rectification that takes place between soulmates. This suggests that soulmates are not just meant to love each other, but also to help each other grow spiritually and fulfill their divine purpose.

Real-life Example: "***Rabbi Akiva and Rachel***"
Rabbi Akiva, one of the greatest sages in Jewish history, was deeply devoted to his wife, Rachel. Before they married, Rachel saw the potential in Akiva, who was then an uneducated shepherd, and encouraged him to pursue his studies. Akiva eventually became a renowned scholar, and he attributed much of his success to Rachel's unwavering support and belief in him. Their story is often cited as an example of a deep, spiritual connection that transcends the material world.

5. **Buddhism: The Spiritual Journey of Two Souls**

Buddhism doesn't explicitly mention soulmates in the way that other religions do. Instead, it focuses on the concepts of karma, reincarnation, and spiritual awakening. Relationships in Buddhism are seen as opportunities for spiritual growth, and the idea of a soulmate is understood as someone who helps you along the path to enlightenment.

Buddhist teachings emphasize the importance of compassion, loving-kindness, and mindfulness in relationships. A true spiritual partnership is one in which both individuals support each other's journey toward awakening. This concept aligns with the idea of soulmates being companions on the spiritual path, helping each other overcome obstacles and achieve inner peace.

Real-life Example: "***Siddhartha and Yasodhara***"
The story of Siddhartha (the Buddha) and his wife Yasodhara is a poignant example of a spiritual connection in

Buddhism. After Siddhartha left the palace to seek enlightenment, Yasodhara supported him from afar, even though it meant enduring great personal hardship. When Siddhartha eventually attained enlightenment and returned, Yasodhara also became a follower of his teachings, showing that their bond was not just one of romantic love but also of shared spiritual purpose.

The Modern Search for Soulmates

In today's world, the idea of soulmates continues to evolve. For some, a soulmate is seen as a romantic partner who completes them, while for others, it is someone who helps them grow and become the best version of themselves. The rise of modern psychology, particularly the works of Carl Jung, introduced the idea of the "**anima**" and "**animus**" – the inner masculine and feminine aspects of the psyche – which echo the ancient spiritual concepts of soulmates.

Modern science also explores the concept of deep connections, though it often frames these ideas in terms of psychology and neuroscience rather than spirituality. For example, the phenomenon of "mirror neurons" suggests that we are wired for empathy and connection, which might explain why certain relationships feel so profoundly resonant.

Real-life Example: "***Johnny Cash and June Carter***"
The love story of Johnny Cash and June Carter is a modern example of a soulmate connection that defied the odds. Both

had complex personal histories, but when they found each other, their connection became a source of strength and redemption. Their relationship was far from perfect, but it was marked by deep love, respect, and mutual support. Even through the challenges of addiction, fame, and personal struggles, they remained devoted to each other until the end.

The Soulmate Connection: A Universal Truth

After exploring the many religious and cultural perspectives on soulmates, it becomes clear that this concept is a universal one. Whether seen as a divine plan, a karmic bond, or a spiritual partnership, the idea of soulmates speaks to a fundamental human truth: we are not meant to journey through life alone. We are meant to connect, to love, and to grow together with others.

Old soulmates version: The story of Prophet Ibrahim (Abraham), his wife Sarah, and his second wife Hagar is a profound example of love, faith, human complexity, and the insecurities that can emerge even among those closest to God. This family dynamic laid the groundwork for religious traditions that have shaped history for over 4,000 years, and at its heart is a story of human emotions that resonate deeply to this day.

The Story of Ibrahim, Sarah, and Hagar

Prophet Ibrahim, revered in Judaism, Christianity, and Islam, was married to Sarah, who is considered the matriarch of the Jewish faith through their son, Isaac (Ishaq). For many years, Sarah was unable to bear children, which was a source of deep pain and insecurity for her. In that era, being childless was often seen as a personal failure, intensifying Sarah's feelings of inadequacy and insecurity in her marriage. As time passed and her hopes of motherhood faded, she encouraged Ibrahim to take, Hagar daughter of the Egyptian Pharaoh, as a second wife so that he could have descendants.

Hagar bore Ibrahim a son, Ismail (Ishmael), who is considered a forefather of the Islamic tradition. Although this arrangement fulfilled Ibrahim's longing for an heir, it intensified Sarah's insecurities, even after she later bore her own son, Ishaq (Isaac). The coexistence of two women and two sons, each with their own place in Ibrahim's life, inevitably created tensions. Out of jealousy and fear that Ismail might overshadow Isaac in his father's heart and legacy, Sarah's resentment grew. Eventually, these emotions led her to demand that Hagar and her son leave.

Ibrahim, deeply pained, complied with Sarah's request after receiving guidance from God. He sent Hagar and Ismail to the desert, where, according to Islamic tradition, they miraculously survived and were blessed by God. Over time, Ismail grew into the forefather of the Arab peoples, and his descendants became central to the lineage of Islam, while Isaac's descendants became foundational to Judaism. Both sons were loved by Ibrahim, yet their separation and the divisions between their descendants would grow into a complex, often conflicted, relationship over the millennia.

The Complexity of Women's Insecurities and Its Lasting Impact

Sarah and Hagar's story illustrates timeless themes of human complexity, especially regarding women's insecurities and how they can affect family dynamics and even shape history. Sarah's initial insecurity over her barrenness and her later jealousy of Hagar were natural, deeply human responses. In the context of their society, her worth and identity were inextricably linked to her role as a mother, which led her to act out of fear when that role seemed threatened.

This dynamic between Sarah and Hagar highlights the struggle between security and insecurity, love and jealousy, and trust and rivalry—emotions that are universal but particularly impactful when they unfold in close relationships. Sarah's fear of losing her husband's.

The story of Abla and Antar is one of the most celebrated and enduring love tales in Arab history and literature, symbolizing the concept of soulmates who remain deeply connected despite immense hardships and societal obstacles. Their story reflects a bond rooted in loyalty, courage, and a profound emotional connection that has inspired generations.

The Story of Abla and Antar: A Love Beyond Boundaries

Antarah ibn Shaddad, known as Antar, was a legendary pre-Islamic Arab poet and warrior. Born to a noble father and an enslaved Ethiopian mother, Antar grew up as an outsider, facing prejudice due to his mixed heritage and his enslaved status within his tribe, the Banu Abs. Despite his struggles, he became a renowned poet and warrior, known for his bravery and strength on the battlefield.

Abla, the daughter of a noble family in his tribe, was the love of Antar's life. She was beautiful, intelligent, and highly esteemed within her tribe, embodying the virtues of nobility and honor. Antar admired Abla from afar, his love for her woven into his poetry, where he described her grace, beauty, and the joy she brought to his heart. His verses became famous, immortalizing his devotion to Abla and establishing his place in the pantheon of Arab literature.

Despite his love for Abla, Antar faced immense obstacles in pursuing her. His status as the son of an enslaved woman was a significant social barrier, and Abla's family was reluctant to accept his proposal due to his background. Yet Antar did not waver; he was determined to prove his worthiness. His love for Abla inspired him to achieve greatness, to fight in battles, and to earn a reputation as a fearless warrior. Antar believed that only through courage and honor could he be worthy of Abla, a love that was as challenging as it was transformative.

Soulmates Against All Odds

Abla and Antar's story is a powerful example of soulmates whose love transcended societal expectations and personal hardships. Despite the social stigma Antar faced, Abla saw him for his true worth—his courage, his loyalty, and the purity of his love for her. She admired him not for his status but for his character and the strength of his devotion. In return, Antar's love for Abla drove him to become a better man, transforming him from a marginalized figure into one of the most celebrated warriors and poets of his time.

The trials that Abla and Antar faced highlight the concept of soulmates as individuals whose connection brings out the best in each other, inspiring mutual growth and resilience. Antar's poetry, often centered on Abla, reflected his soul's longing and his heart's steadfast commitment to her, even when faced with insurmountable odds.

He wrote verses about the battles he fought, not only for honor but as proof of his devotion, with the hope that one day he might be deemed worthy of her hand.

The Depth of Their Connection

Abla and Antar's love endured through separation, societal scorn, and even war. Their relationship illustrates how soulmates share a connection that is not solely dependent on being physically together but is sustained through mutual respect, unwavering loyalty, and a deep emotional bond.

Antar's poems about Abla were not just expressions of romantic love; they were testaments to a love that defied boundaries. Through his words, he declared her his soulmate, the one who completed him, inspired him, and gave his life meaning.

One of Antar's famous lines expresses his intense love and yearning for Abla:

> *"My heart is captive to her love, and my soul clings to her as if she were the very breath I need to live."*

For Antar, Abla was not just a beloved; she was his guiding light and the source of his strength. His poetry often portrayed her as the reason behind his bravery, a beacon of hope in a world that tried to keep them apart. Abla, in turn, accepted Antar's love with grace and devotion, recognizing the purity of his heart, even if society did not.

A Legacy of Love

The story of Abla and Antar has endured for centuries, symbolizing the idea that true love knows no bounds. Their story is celebrated not just for its romance but for the way it transcends the limitations imposed by society. Their love represents the power of connection that sees beyond the superficial and cherishes the soul, embodying the Arab ideal of undying loyalty and devotion.

In a world that did not easily allow them to be together, Abla and Antar's love became an immortal legend, illustrating that soulmates are those who find each other against all odds, who inspire each other to grow, and whose love leaves an impact on the world long after they are gone.

What is most remarkable about the concept of soulmates is its ability to transcend the individual. While the romantic notion of a soulmate is powerful, the spiritual truth goes beyond just two people in love. It encompasses the idea of connection in all its forms – between friends, family members, teachers, and students. Soulmates are those who touch our souls, who challenge us, and who inspire us to become more than we are.

In this sense, the journey of finding a soulmate is not just about finding "the one" but about recognizing and cherishing the soul connections we make throughout our lives.

These connections, whether they last a lifetime or just a moment, are the threads that weave the fabric of our existence.

Conclusion: The Eternal Dance of Souls

As we conclude this journey, we are reminded that the search for a soulmate is not just about seeking another person; it is about seeking ourselves. In ourselves. In the quest for a soulmate, we are often drawn into a deeper understanding of who we are and what we seek in life. The soulmate relationship, whether romantic, platonic, or spiritual, is ultimately about growth, transformation, and the realization of our fullest potential. It's about finding someone who mirrors our soul, challenging us to confront our fears, embrace our strengths, and evolve.

Soulmates, in many traditions, are seen as guides, partners who accompany us on our spiritual journey. They are not merely a source of comfort but also catalysts for change. Through their presence in our lives, we learn lessons we might never have encountered on our own. This is why the concept of a soulmate is so deeply intertwined with the idea of destiny and purpose.

Embracing the Soulmate Connection

In understanding the nature of soulmates, we must also recognize that these connections are not always easy. They may challenge us in ways we never anticipated. A soulmate relationship can be marked by intense joy, but also by profound struggle. This struggle, however, is often where the greatest growth occurs. It pushes us to confront our shadows and insecurities and, through this confrontation, to become more aligned with our true selves.

In every tradition, from the passionate love of Radha and Krishna in Hinduism to the divine partnership of Prophet Muhammad and Khadijah in Islam, to the divine partnership of Prophet Ibrahim with his first wife Sarah and second wife

Hajar in old time, to the divine partnership of Abla & Antar in Arab world, soulmates are depicted as those who help us navigate the complexities of life. They reflect back to us our truest selves, often in ways that are both beautiful and painful. It is in this reflection that we find the opportunity for healing and transformation.

The soulmate connection, therefore, is not about perfection. It is about two imperfect people who come together to create something extraordinary. It is about recognizing that love, in all its forms, is a path to spiritual awakening. Through love, we learn patience, kindness, forgiveness, and resilience. Through love, we are reminded of our shared humanity and our divine nature.

The Global Tapestry of Soulmates

As we explore the idea of soulmates across cultures, we see that this concept is truly universal. From the predestined "bashert" in Judaism to the karmic bonds of Hinduism, the soulmate connection transcends religious boundaries. It speaks to something fundamental about the human experience: our innate desire for connection, for unity, for love.

Even in modern psychology, the idea of a "soulmate" has evolved into discussions about emotional and psychological compatibility. Terms like "twin flame" and "mirror soul" have entered popular discourse, suggesting that these relationships are not just about romantic attraction but about deep spiritual resonance.

In every corner of the world, stories of soulmates persist because they speak to the timeless truth that we are all connected. Whether through divine intervention, karmic ties, or shared destiny, soulmates remind us that we are never truly alone in this journey.

Real-life Example: "***John Lennon and Yoko Ono***"
One of the most famous soulmate pairings of the 20th century, John Lennon and Yoko Ono shared a deep artistic and spiritual bond. Their relationship was unconventional and often controversial, but it was undeniably powerful. They inspired and challenged each other, using their love to create art, music, and social change. Despite public scrutiny, their connection was a testament to the idea that soulmates are not just lovers but collaborators on a shared mission.

Beyond Romance: The Many Faces of Soulmates

While the concept of soulmates is often associated with romantic love, it's important to recognize that soulmates come in many forms. They can be friends, family members, mentors, or even strangers who come into our lives for a brief but impactful moment. Each of these connections serves a purpose, helping us to grow, heal, and evolve.

For instance, the bond between best friends can be just as profound as a romantic connection. These friendships, which often span decades, are built on trust, mutual understanding, and unconditional support. They are soul connections that enrich our lives in ways that go beyond the romantic ideal.

In some cases, a soulmate may come into our lives for a short period, leaving a lasting impact. These brief encounters can teach us valuable lessons, helping us to navigate our personal and spiritual journey. The soulmate connection, therefore, is not limited to lifelong partnerships; it is about recognizing the significance of every soul we encounter along the way.

Real-life Example: "***Oprah Winfrey and Gayle King***"
The friendship between Oprah Winfrey and Gayle King is an example of a non-romantic soulmate connection. Their bond, which spans over four decades, has been marked by mutual support, love, and understanding. Both have credited their friendship as one of the most important relationships in their lives, demonstrating that soulmates can be found in friendships that offer profound emotional and spiritual support.

The Spiritual Evolution of Soulmates

As we conclude this exploration, it's important to remember that the journey with a soulmate is not just about finding love or companionship; it is about spiritual evolution. Soulmates help us to awaken to our true selves, guiding us through the highs and lows of life. They push us to grow, to change, and to become the best version of ourselves.

In this way, the soulmate connection is ultimately a path to self-realization. It is about more than just finding someone to share our life with; it is about finding someone who helps us to discover who we truly are. The soulmate, in this sense, is a mirror, reflecting back to us both our light and our shadows.

Real-life Example: "***Mahatma Gandhi and Kasturba Gandhi***" The relationship between Mahatma Gandhi and his wife, Kasturba, was a partnership that transcended the personal and entered the realm of spiritual evolution. Kasturba supported Gandhi through his journey of nonviolent resistance, often at great personal sacrifice. Their relationship was one of mutual respect, shared values, and a deep commitment to a higher purpose. Together, they worked not only for their personal fulfillment but for the liberation and betterment of others.

The Soulmate Concept in LGBT Relationships

The concept of soulmates holds a universal appeal: it's the idea of finding someone who understands, completes, and inspires us in profound ways. For many people, this notion of a soulmate can transcend traditional boundaries, including gender. However, the idea of LGBT relationships, especially same-sex partnerships, is complex and often met with various reactions depending on cultural, religious, and personal beliefs.

In LGBT relationships, the idea of a soulmate can feel just as powerful, if not more so, because many individuals within the community may have felt misunderstood or out of place.

Finding a partner who accepts, understands, and complements them becomes a powerful experience of validation and love. Just like heterosexual relationships, LGBT relationships can be based on deep emotional connection, mutual respect, and an understanding that goes beyond surface-level compatibility.

The confusion often arises because traditional views of soulmates are rooted in heteronormative perspectives. Many religious and cultural beliefs see a soulmate as the completion of two complementary energies, typically viewed as masculine and feminine, that come together to form a balanced whole. LGBT soulmates, however, challenge this perspective by showing that soul connections can exist between any two people, regardless of gender, and that love is not limited by traditional notions of gender roles.

Why Religion Often Refuses LGBT Relationships

Many religious traditions, particularly those stemming from Abrahamic religions like Judaism, Christianity, and Islam, have historically opposed same-sex relationships. This opposition often stems from interpretations of sacred texts, longstanding doctrines, and the cultural contexts in which these religions emerged.

Here's a closer look at some reasons:

1. **Scriptural Interpretations:** Many religious texts contain passages that have been interpreted as prohibiting same-sex relationships. For example, certain verses in the Torah, Bible, and Quran are cited as condemning homosexual acts. These texts were written in times when social structures, family lineage, and population growth were priorities, influencing their stances on relationships and reproduction.
2. **Traditional Views on Gender Roles:** Religious teachings have often emphasized distinct, complementary roles for men and women. In this view, a "soulmate" relationship is often seen as a union between two people with distinct roles that together fulfill a natural or divine order. LGBT relationships, by this view, are seen as incompatible with the traditional balance of masculine and feminine energies.
3. **Moral and Social Order:** Many religions prioritize preserving a social order that aligns with their teachings. Some leaders see LGBT relationships as a threat to traditional family structures, often viewed as the foundation of society. This leads to a preference for

relationships that align with traditional norms, and LGBT relationships may be seen as conflicting with this ideal.

4. **Fear of Change and Cultural Identity:** Religious communities sometimes resist LGBT acceptance out of concern that such changes could dilute or alter their cultural and spiritual identity. There can be a fear that changing views on relationships could disrupt long-standing traditions or compromise beliefs central to the faith.

The Confusion and Complexity

For LGBT individuals of faith, this creates a deeply challenging situation. They may feel a genuine connection to their spirituality and want to remain true to their beliefs, yet they also feel a powerful, authentic love or identity that the religion doesn't accept. This can lead to feelings of guilt, isolation, or confusion as they try to reconcile their faith with their experiences and emotions.

There is also confusion because views on sexuality, gender, and relationships have evolved rapidly in recent decades, and many people now view gender and love as fluid, personal experiences. This evolution can create tension within religious communities where traditional views are held, and where newer perspectives are seen as conflicting with foundational beliefs.

The Ongoing Conversation

In recent years, many religious communities have begun to revisit these issues, engaging in discussions around love, acceptance, and understanding. Some branches of religions have found ways to embrace LGBT individuals, focusing on the core values of compassion, love, and the belief that God's love is universal. While change is gradual, these conversations represent an ongoing journey toward reconciling tradition with the diversity of human experiences.

Conclusion

The concept of soulmates is universal, yet how we interpret it can vary widely based on culture, religion, and individual beliefs. LGBT relationships challenge traditional religious views by showing that deep, soul-connected love is not exclusive to heterosexual relationships. As society continues to explore and understand the spectrum of human relationships, we see both tensions and dialogues within religious communities regarding LGBT inclusion. This reflects a world in which people are continually trying to balance the principles of faith with the realities of diverse human experiences.

Talbina: A Healing Food Recommended by the Prophet Muhammad (PBUH) to heal the broken heart.

A Healing Food Recommended by the Prophet Muhammad (PBUH) - Talbina is a simple, nourishing dish made from barley that Prophet Muhammad (PBUH) recommended for its calming and healing properties. He described it as a remedy to soothe the heart and ease sorrow. Talbina is often recommended for those experiencing grief, stress, or emotional pain, including the pain that comes from love or loss. It's a comforting food rich in nutrients, with a gentle texture that many find grounding and calming.

Ingredients

The traditional ingredients for talbina are simple and wholesome:

- Barley flour: 1–2 tablespoons (you can also use whole barley or ground barley for added texture)
- Milk or water: 1 cup (milk adds a creamier consistency and extra nutrients)
- Honey: 1–2 teaspoons (to taste, for natural sweetness and added health benefits)
- Optional spices: cinnamon, cardamom, or saffron (for flavor and added calming properties)

Preparation Method

1. **Mix the barley flour and milk (or water):** In a small pot, gradually mix the barley flour with milk or water to avoid lumps.
2. **Cook on low heat:** Place the mixture over low heat, stirring constantly. Cook for about 10–

15 minutes until it reaches a thick, porridge-like consistency.

3. **Sweeten with honey:** Remove from heat, and stir in honey to taste. Add a pinch of cinnamon, cardamom, or saffron if desired.
4. **Serve warm:** Pour into a bowl and serve warm, as warmth adds to its comforting and soothing effect.

How to Eat Talbina to Heal the Heart

Eating talbina mindfully can be a comforting ritual, especially when dealing with emotional pain, such as heartache or grief. Here are some ways to make the experience more healing:

1. Eat slowly and mindfully: Focus on each bite, savoring the warmth and gentle flavors. This allows you to fully receive the nourishing qualities of the food.
2. Reflect on healing intentions: As you eat, remind yourself of Prophet Muhammad's words about talbina as a comfort for sadness. Set an intention to let go of pain and welcome peace.
3. Incorporate it into a calming routine: Eat talbina during a quiet time of the day, perhaps as a morning ritual or in the evening, paired with calming activities like reading, reflection, or prayer.

Benefits of Talbina for Emotional Well-being

1. **Nutritional benefits:** Barley is rich in fiber, vitamins (especially B vitamins), and minerals, all of which support mood and mental health.
2. Gentle on digestion: Its soft, porridge-like texture is easy to digest, which can be particularly soothing during emotional turmoil when stress may affect appetite or digestion.
3. **Natural serotonin booster:** Barley contains tryptophan, an amino acid that helps produce serotonin, a hormone that promotes feelings of calm and well-being.
4. **Tradition of healing:** Eating a food with a long-standing tradition of healing, recommended by the Prophet, can bring a sense of spiritual connection and comfort.

Talbina is more than just a food; it's a reminder of the compassionate wisdom in the Sunnah, guiding us toward gentle and nourishing ways to care for ourselves in times of emotional need.

Final Reflections: Embracing the Soulmate Journey

In the end, the search for a soulmate is a deeply personal and spiritual journey. It is a journey that invites us to look within and to seek connection with others in meaningful and transformative ways. Whether we find our soulmate in a partner, a friend, or even within ourselves, the experience of deep, soulful connection is one of the most profound aspects of the human experience. The soulmate journey is not always easy, but it is always worthwhile. It reminds us of our capacity for love, for growth, and for spiritual awakening. It challenges us to be vulnerable, to be brave, and to trust in the power of connection. And, ultimately, it teaches us that the greatest love of all is the love that leads us back to ourselves. As we close this chapter, may you be inspired to embrace the soulmate connections in your life – past, present, and future. May you recognize the beauty of these relationships, not only in their moments of joy but also in their moments of challenge. For it is through these connections that we come to understand the true nature of love, and the true purpose of our souls.

Endnotes

In the diverse spiritual and religious traditions explored, the concept of soulmates reveals itself as a universal truth. Whether viewed through the lens of divine destiny, karmic bonds, or spiritual partnership, the soulmate connection transcends boundaries and touches the very essence of what it means to be human.

We are all on this journey together, and it is through our relationships – our soulmates – that we find meaning, purpose, and love. As you continue your own journey, may you be open to the soul connections that await you, and may you find the courage to embrace the lessons they bring.

Chapter 2

Embracing The Feminine Enigma

Abstract Introduction

How does one truly capture the heart of a man?

Do you wish to have a man wholly devoted, wrapped around your finger? You may be surprised to learn that the answer is simpler than one might assume. Women, by nature, often bring complexity into relationships, while men, conversely, lean toward simplicity. This difference in approach can create misunderstandings, especially in our modern era, where relationships often seem more fleeting than ever, despite advances in communication. Have you ever pondered, "Why did relationships of the past seem to hold deeper love, longing, and passion, while today's instant connectivity often leaves us feeling more distant?"

In many male-dominated societies, particularly within Arab regions, relationships face unique dynamics. This book seeks to be your ultimate guide to understanding men, providing insights to captivate the heart of any man, whether he appears to be an easy catch or a formidable challenge. Men differ widely in personality, social standing, education, and wealth, yet they all share a core response to certain traits in women. This guide is not crafted from mere observation or casual opinion but rather grounded in genuine insights drawn from a diverse spectrum of men experiences —from the refined to the rebellious, from the straightforward to the deceptive, from the self-assured to those yet finding their way. In the end, all men, regardless of character, hold a common perception of the qualities in a woman that draw them close and kindle lasting affection.

The truth remains: women are often drawn to men of strong character who maintain their dignity, even if such men might break their hearts. Yet, paradoxically, a man who sets aside his pride to love with unreserved devotion may gain her loyalty, but at times, she may take his love for granted, seeking instead the thrill of challenge. Human nature craves excitement over predictability, and this applies to both men and women alike. If this reflects a woman's mindset, then how might a man feel, knowing he too is drawn toward the excitement of pursuit over the assurance of certainty?

This book delves into the timeless dance of attraction and affection, unveiling the nuances that bridge these desires.

Ring on His Finger (genuine, kind-hearted, and straightforward in her intentions "pure-hearted girl"), Ring on Mine (clever, self-assured and subtly manipulative "devil girl")

FIRST EXAMPLE:

In case of "pure-hearted girl":

He says, "Don't go out without a reason; just say 'God willing' and stay home," while he's out enjoying himself with friends, feeling proud to have a young woman who listens to him.

In case of "devil girl":

When he says, "Don't go out," you reply with a pleasant, "Of course, God willing." Sometimes you genuinely don't feel like going out, so you stay in; other times, you decide to go out anyway, standing your ground if he protests without a valid reason.

SECOND EXAMPLE:

In case of "pure-hearted girl":

He tells you, "Don't wear that, don't dress up, don't put on anything," and you answer sweetly, "As you wish." To him, you appear accommodating and agreeable.

In case of "devil girl":

He says, "Don't put on makeup," and you respond with, "As you wish, my love," yet when you're with your friends, you live freely, while he remains blissfully unaware.

THIRD EXAMPLE:

In case of "pure-hearted girl":

When he's upset without any reason, you try endlessly to calm him down, blaming yourself, apologizing, and setting aside everything until his mood improves.

In case of "devil girl":
When he's upset without any reason, you say Let's talk when you're ready to be kind." Sometimes, you even end the call aside not acknowledging his mood.

FORTH EXAMPLE:
In case of "pure-hearted girl":
If he's in a bad mood and vents his frustration on you, you keep your calm, letting him manage his own emotions until he comes around.

In case of "devil girl":
When he's frustrated by something outside your relationship and takes it out on you, you calmly say, "Let's talk when you're ready to be kind." Sometimes, you even end the call, giving him space to sort out his own mood.

FIFTH EXAMPLE:
In case of "pure-hearted girl":
If he calls last minute saying, "Shall we go out?" you say, "Of course, darling, I'll wait for you," canceling all your plans and feeling a rush of excitement like a girl on her first date.

In case of "devil girl":
Or, he calls at the last moment suggesting to go out, and you say, "I can't, I wish you'd told me sooner. Let's plan for another day, God willing—or go out if you have free time, and we'll catch up soon."

At the beginning of a relationship, friends and close ones might advise you, "Ignore him. Let him go… ignore… Men love a challenge." But hold on! He's only just getting to know you—he hasn't experienced your personality or spontaneity yet. Sure, you might think, "That advice is outdated," but the best approach to follow is "Be gentle until you get the hang of it." There's wisdom here: don't let minor things upset you, and if they do, keep it to yourself at first. Early on, a man may not appreciate grumpiness or heavy sadness; he hasn't fallen in love deeply enough yet to want to weather your moods. But once he's hooked, that's when things change, and even your sadness can become endearing to him.

A man loves a woman who is joyful, at peace, and cares for herself. Why does this attract him? Because she's showing him that life with her will be uplifting and fulfilling. Her self-love and confidence draw others in, and he sees her as someone intelligent and vibrant, sensing that her positive energy will enrich him, too. In the end, everyone wants happiness—with just a hint of mystery!

Types of Men

A man is often like a big kid—understanding him can sometimes be simple, yet it's often women who unintentionally make it more complex. Ultimately, most men are drawn to a woman who is a storyteller, someone who brings life to conversation. However, when a woman seems insincere or too eager to share every feeling, a man may sense a lack of trustworthiness and feel unsettled. On the other hand, a woman who's steady, confident, and secure in her feelings gives a man the assurance that her love is reliable and enduring. When it comes to understanding men, there are generally four types of personalities to consider. Let's explore the first:

The "Charming Valley"

This type of man is smooth-talking and charismatic, knowing exactly what to say and how to say it. He has studied interactions carefully, understanding what different women want to hear and how to respond to each. He's got a knack for charm and carries himself with confidence. Adam, for instance, is a young man blessed with good looks and natural charisma. Even though he might not be wealthy, he has a magnetic quality—he seems to effortlessly capture the heart of any woman he meets. It's as if his charm alone makes every girl he sets his eyes on fall for him.

Whether it's a casual encounter or a serious interest, the typical scenario in Adam's life goes like this:

1. He notices a girl in a public place and is drawn to her.
2. He takes the initiative, makes his admiration clear, and waits for her to reach out.
3. She enters Adam's world, completely unaware of his true intentions.

4. He makes her feel like she's the only one who's ever captivated him.
5. He doesn't rush or overwhelm her; instead, he gives her space to feel at ease.
6. He tells her, "I know what you like and what's on your mind," showing that he's been searching for someone just like her.
7. He goes along with her desires, coming across as incredibly sweet and charming, quickly finding a place in her heart.
8. Even his friends join in, telling her, "What did you do to him? He only talks about you!" (A line every girl who gets close to Adam has heard).
9. The girl believes in this love story, getting deeply attached, unaware that it's one-sided.
10. Once he's gotten what he wanted, he leaves, off in search of a new interest/victim.

And so the cycle continues.

The Romantic Man

This is the ideal partner every girl dreams of but rarely finds. A true romantic man is someone who not only speaks sweet words but also follows them with actions. He's the dream partner, genuine in both words and deeds. Every girl deserves someone like this, so look for him—or if you're with someone now, help bring out his romantic side with your strength and cleverness. Don't settle for less; you deserve a love that is expressed both in actions and in words.

Take the story of Sarah and Adam, a couple in a wonderfully healthy and rare relationship. Adam is charming and adventurous. Before meeting Sarah, he was carefree and independent. Many women he dated tried to control him or win his affection by any means, but they never succeeded. Then Sarah entered his life, and she inspired a transformation. Adam, who had always kept his distance, became her true romantic. He showed his love not only through words but also through genuine actions.

For example, Adam had never been one to attend Sunday prayers regularly, but Sarah brought it up casually one day, saying with a smile, "I find men who don't attend Sunday prayers oddly attractive," and then she moved on without waiting for his response. Two weeks later, Adam began attending Sunday prayers at the Church. He would tell her, "Sarah, you're my happiness, and everything I do now, I love doing it with you. I've never felt this way before, but something about your spontaneity and strength just draws me in. It's like you don't even have to try…"

Through her genuine, confident presence, Sarah brought out the best in Adam, and he became her true romantic, proving his love in both words and actions. You satisfy me in everything that made me attracted to you, even though I wasn't supposed to tell you this. It's very strange for a man to admit this dangerous confession, which is the weak point of any man. If you want Romeo, think of what pleases you, but he also thinks of pleasing you.

The Stoic Man

The stoic man is someone who appears tough and unbothered on the outside, but his feelings run deep beneath the surface. He may love you intensely, even be willing to go to great lengths for you, yet he hides it, acting as if he's indifferent. Many have encountered or will encounter this type of man—the opposite of the expressive, sweet-talking guy. He doesn't verbalize his emotions, but his actions reveal his loyalty and devotion.

Take James, for instance. He's a humble, kind-hearted young man, yet he's always wanted to project a tougher, more confident image—the one who's always in control, who "knows what's up." James met Deborah and fell for her almost instantly. Deborah, being playful and clever, sensed his feelings and often teased him, fully aware of the effect she had on him. James, however, kept his emotions hidden, shyly avoiding direct conversations about his feelings.

One day, Deborah spontaneously asked, "James, do you love me?" Caught off guard, James grew tense and nervously replied, "Love you? Why would I love you? I respect you, sure, but love? No, I don't love you!" Deborah didn't respond but was inwardly amused and even more convinced of his feelings. She knew that despite his words, his actions showed his genuine care—he was always willing to go the extra mile for her without hesitation, even though he'd never admit it outright.

In the end, Deborah realized his love was unspoken but steadfast, a devotion that showed itself not in words but in the countless things he did for her, quietly and consistently.

Mama's Boy

This guy—let's not even call him a "man"—is more like a boy, with a weak personality and no real sense of independence. Often under the sway of a controlling, narcissistic parent or a narcissist friend, he lacks the strength to make his own choices and hasn't developed the ability to stand on his own. This boy is hardly a decision-maker; he's always living under his mother's influence, unable to make even the smallest decision without her approval.

In today's world, many women are independent and decisive, often supported by their mothers to live fulfilling, autonomous lives. But if a man can't step out of his mother's shadow, especially one cast by a parent with a need for control, how can he make choices or build a genuine partnership? Unfortunately, there are many men in society who fall into this category, letting their lives be dictated by a dominant mother under the misconception of "parental consent." Parental consent is important, but it doesn't mean sacrificing all personal agency. Everyone should have their own identity, able to communicate, compromise, and ultimately choose what's best for them.

The worst type of "mama's boy" is the one who lets his mother choose his life partner, leading to inevitable issues:

- **Lack of Independence:** Under the influence of a narcissistic parent, he doesn't know how to make his own decisions, relying on his mother for everything, making him unreliable as a partner.
- **No Personal Goals:** He doesn't know what he wants; he only knows what his controlling parent wants, so he ends up living according to her tastes and preferences.
- **Shallow Commitment to Marriage:** He's more invested in the idea of marriage than in the person he'll spend his life with, prioritizing his mother's happiness over his own.
- **Trust Issues:** His partner can't fully trust him because he lacks confidence and self-assurance, making it impossible for her to feel secure.
- **A Third Person in the Marriage:** His mother remains a constant third presence in the relationship, exerting control and creating a dynamic where his wife feels she's married not just to him but to his mother as well.

Ultimately, this type of relationship leaves his partner feeling isolated and disconnected. She finds herself in a marriage with a handsome but dependent man, overshadowed by a controlling parent who dominates their lives. When his mother's influence leads to unhappiness, she rarely admits her mistake, leaving him and his partner to bear the consequences, unable to break free from the cycle of dependency and control.

Ahmed was a handsome, well-mannered man, and he was in a relationship with a girl he had met at in a restaurant named Nivin. Nivin was sophisticated, respectful, and carried herself with grace. Ahmed's mother knew about their relationship, and one day, both women found themselves at the same wedding. When Nivin saw Ahmed's mother, she warmly approached her and greeted her.

However, after that encounter, Ahmed's mother began to feel a growing unease, fearing that Nivin might one day "take her son away." She thought to herself, "If he doesn't choose her, then he won't choose her—I'll make sure of it." Although Ahmed's mother couldn't find a single flaw in Nivin, her issue was precisely that Nivin was perfect. This was the beginning of her motherly jealousy, as she began to place her own feelings above her son's happiness.

Determined, Ahmed's mother decided to confront him directly. "Nivin is not the one you will marry," she declared firmly. What do you think Ahmed, raised to be obedient and respectful, did in response? True to his nature, he didn't question her. Days passed, and Ahmed's mother selected a woman she deemed more "suitable" for the family. Overjoyed, she was confident in her choice, and Ahmed felt obligated to follow her wishes, even though he sensed she might be wrong.

His new fiancée was kind-hearted, gentle, and undemanding during their engagement, accepting the arrangement with the best intentions.

But after the marriage, reality hit hard. Ahmed's mother, once thrilled with her choice, soon faced disappointment. Living together with her new daughter-in-law, she saw firsthand that things weren't as she had hoped. Ahmed's wife, who had initially accepted living with his mother, became increasingly independent and distant. She came and went from the house as if Ahmed's mother didn't exist, paying little regard to her wishes or presence.

This turn of events left Ahmed's mother frustrated and bewildered, realizing that her interference had created a situation she could no longer control. Ahmed's new wife began to show her true colors, paying no regard to his mother. She wouldn't even greet her mother-in-law, ignoring her presence entirely. Soon, her demands started pouring in: "I want the latest model car… I want my own house… I want to travel… I want this designer bag!" Ahmed, as we've said, felt powerless, carrying out her demands without question.

Ahmed's mother, who had once felt so in control, was now tongue-tied, unable to complain—after all, she had brought this situation upon herself. Regret began to creep in, and she started to think of Nivin, sighing, "If only it had been Nivin… If only I hadn't stubbornly stood in my son's way."

Eventually, she confronted Ahmed, expressing her frustration over his wife's disregard for her and the strain on the family. His response was blunt: "You're the one who chose her, so deal with it, may God protect you."

And there it was—Ahmed's mother, who had once been so determined to control his life, now found herself facing the consequences of her own choices. In the end, her "perfect" plan had turned against her, showing that sometimes, forcing a choice can lead to unexpcted disasters.

The Devil's Daughter and the Pure-Hearted "Village" Girl – Are You a Village Girl?

Let's see if you might be the "village pure-hearted girl" type—someone often taken for granted and overlooked by men. Here, "village girl" doesn't refer to a rural upbringing but instead symbolizes innocence and naivety. Answer the following questions, and if you say "yes" more often than "no," you may find yourself fitting this role.

1. Do you cancel plans with friends at the last minute to be with him?
2. Do you sacrifice your own comfort, like losing sleep, to talk to him?
3. Do you set alarms to make yourself available for him, even if it means only getting a few hours of rest?
4. Do you say "yes" to everything he asks without fully understanding why?

5. Has he managed to convince you to compromise on things that matter to you, just to keep him happy?
6. Do you give in easily to his desires?
7. Do you feel guilty when you say "no" to him, even if you know you're right?
8. Has he persuaded you to spend money on him, making you feel as though you share everything financially?
9. When you need help, do you hesitate to ask him, fearing it might burden him?
10. If he upsets you or speaks rudely, do you avoid showing how you feel?
11. Do you put up with going to places you don't enjoy, just to make him comfortable?

If you answered "**yes**" to most of these, it's time to reflect.

Now, what's the main difference between the "village girl" and the "devil's daughter"? The reality, as many have learned, is that men are naturally drawn to the "devil's daughter" type. Here's a truth we've discovered through experience and careful observation: a man's secret, often unacknowledged, is his attraction to the woman who challenges him.

A man, born as hunter, tends to approach relationships logically. So why is he drawn to a woman who keeps him on his toes? Quite simply, because she doesn't make it easy for him, doesn't drain him with constant demands, and allows him to chase her. In contrast, the "village girl" is a sure thing; she loves him unconditionally, always forgives, and doesn't make him wonder or worry. This leads him to take her for granted, and while he may love and appreciate her, the excitement and depth are often missing.

The Village Girl is the woman who:

- Over-sacrifices, putting her partner's needs above her own.
- Prioritizes him over her family, giving everything to make him happy.
- Cares less about herself, often neglecting her own needs.
- Believes her partner is "perfect" despite any faults, blaming herself if things go wrong.
- Feels grateful for the small gestures he does, while excusing any disrespect.

Men appreciate the loyalty and comfort of the "village girl," but they often seek out the "devil's daughter" for excitement and intrigue. The Devil's Daughter is the one every man secretly desires but may never admit. She's confident, mysterious, and keeps him guessing. Like a falcon, she knows her goals and isn't afraid to pursue them. When life brings her down, she bounces back quickly, never allowing herself to be the victim. Because of her self-assured nature, people feel compelled to prove their loyalty to her.

Traits of the Devil's Daughter:

- Loves herself deeply, often being accused of selfishness, yet people are drawn to her.

- Makes a man feel like she's an investment, causing him to give his time, emotions, and even money freely.
- Knows when to be sweet and when to distance herself, keeping him eager and uncertain.
- Is kind in tone but decisive in action, knowing how to subtly control his emotions.
- Treats him as a part of her life, not the center of it, making him long for her attention.
- Spoils him playfully, as a lover would, without ever giving off motherly vibes.
- Balances interest and distance, giving him just enough to make him want more.

The "**village girl**" often keeps a man secure and stable, feeling like she's always there for him. Yet it's the "**devil's daughter**" who leaves a mark on his heart, captivating him with her mystery and strength.

An Insight from an Experienced Voice

We interviewed an influential figure on this topic, who provided a candid view: "The village girl brings peace to the home. She's loyal, grounded, and focused solely on her family. But every man desires the thrill that comes with a 'devil's daughter,' the woman who keeps him interested, aware, and on his toes. That's the difference—one provides stability, the other brings excitement."

In the end, the "**village girl**" might provide the stability men seek in a home and family, while the "**devil's daughter**" brings the excitement, challenge, and mystery men crave in a relationship.

The character of "the daughter of the devil" you've described is incredibly layered, balancing allure, volatility, and an intense, almost intoxicating presence. Let's break down her characteristics:

Personality

1. **Self-Adoring and Self-Reliant:** Her love for herself keeps her perpetually youthful, both in spirit and appearance. She prioritizes her needs, pleasure, and desires, which might seem narcissistic but also fuels her relentless self-development.
2. **Unpredictable and Multi-Faceted:** With 100 "*personalities*," she's ever-changing and never dull. She's adaptable, presenting different facets of herself depending on her mood, which keeps those around her intrigued and guessing. This unpredictability makes her magnetic and infuriating at the same time.
3. **Playful Yet Ruthless:** She's playful with her "*childlike spirit*," yet can be harsh when slighted. Her strength lies in her ability to make her partner feel both irreplaceable and at her mercy. Like a snake shedding skins, she constantly reinvents herself, becoming someone new with each encounter, which

makes her nearly impossible to pin down or predict.

4. **Driven by Freedom and Self-Improvement:** She craves experiences, growth, and knowledge. Rather than settling into societal norms, she's continuously searching, learning, and evolving. Her lack of permanence makes her untouchable—her freedom is her shield.
5. **Dynamic and Elusive:** She pulls people close with warmth and then pushes them away. This creates a cycle of constant pursuit for anyone enchanted by her, ensuring she remains unforgettable. For her, relationships are a game of control and release, where she is both vulnerable and untouchable.

Appearance

1. **Eternal Youthfulness:** Her dedication to self-care, fitness, and beauty keeps her looking younger than her years. Her style is likely bold, a mix of elegance with a bit of mischief, giving her a timeless yet rebellious charm.
2. **Striking, Ever-Changing Style:** Like her personality, her appearance might be chameleon-like, constantly shifting to match her current mood or the person she's interacting with. She could use her looks to accentuate her allure, presenting as

sophisticated or bohemian depending on what effect she desires.

Relationships and Impact on Others

1. **The Roller-Coaster Effect:** To her lovers, she brings both heaven and hell. She's able to create a euphoric high, making her partner feel like royalty, only to flip the switch and take control without warning. Her lovers are left on edge, constantly craving her attention but never certain of her commitment.
2. **An Addiction and a Challenge:** Men find her captivating to the point of obsession, feeling as though they're constantly vying for her attention and approval. She doesn't seek to provide stability—instead, she's a mystery that keeps them forever enthralled, sometimes even sacrificing their own happiness just for the thrill of being with her.
3. **Complicated Attachment:** While she is the center of her lover's world, she herself might feel unattached and independent. Any expression of deep feelings or dependence is met with a cold, sometimes ruthless detachment, serving as a reminder that she will always be an enigma and ultimately untamable.
4. **Reflecting Men's Desires and Weaknesses:** Men see in her what they want to see, and she knows this. By understanding how to hold the

mirror up to their desires, she draws them in and even manipulates them, embodying both what they crave and what they fear.

5. **Emotional Vampirism with a Spark of Redemption:** While she drains those who love her, she also leaves them better, or at least changed, for the experience. She inspires obsession, jealousy, and an undying fascination, but there's also a transformative quality in how she challenges their views on love and life.

Outlook on Life

1. **Rebellion Against Convention:** Her self-awareness allows her to see the traditional "rules" of relationships and life as flexible, or even irrelevant. She sets her own terms and doesn't conform to social expectations, making her both empowering and terrifying to others.
2. **Living for Thrills, Not Promises:** She's drawn to the exhilarating, the immediate, and the tangible rather than distant promises of stability or permanence. Her approach to life is to live in the moment, to prioritize pleasure, self-discovery, and freedom.
3. **Relentless Self-Love as Armor:** Her unwavering self-love is both her strength and her weakness. It keeps her guarded, ensuring

she's never truly vulnerable to others' affections. But this armor makes it difficult for her to experience a genuine connection, ultimately leaving her both liberated and isolated.

Symbolism and Literary Archetype

The daughter of the devil is the embodiment of the femme fatale archetype—a woman whose allure and self-possession make her irresistible yet dangerous. She's a reminder of life's impermanence and unpredictability, challenging those who fall under her spell to abandon stability and embrace the chaos she brings. She forces people to confront their deepest desires and insecurities, creating both passion and turmoil in her wake.

This character would be an ideal anti-heroine, embodying independence, confidence, and self-determination. She's a character whose presence causes upheaval, but whose existence also reveals the depths of the human heart—love, obsession, control, and liberation.

The story of Nigel and the two Mashas illustrates the contrasting nature of selfless devotion and reckless independence in relationships and how each can impact a partner in uniquely intense ways.

The "**daughter of the devil**" archetype embodies both attraction and volatility. She is youthful in spirit, spontaneous, and captivating, often younger in outlook and appearance than her actual age due to her self-assuredness and zest for life. Her life is a thrill, pulling others into a roller coaster of emotional highs and lows. She can be both comforting and controlling, sweet and severe—creating a world of excitement and unpredictability. Her strength lies in her confidence and constant self-evolution, which makes her endlessly fascinating yet a challenge for those who try to anchor her.

In Nigel's life, the two Mashas reveal different aspects of love and attachment. The "**poor**" Masha, who gives everything without expectation, is loyal to the point of self-sacrifice, never allowing herself to impose or control Nigel. She continually gives, not out of need for reciprocation, but out of a desire for his presence, accepting his indifference in exchange for proximity. Her gentleness and acquiescence, however, fail to ignite lasting love in Nigel, who, though appreciative, never truly values her. Instead, his attachment to her is tinged with pity, not passion.

On the other hand, the "**vile**" Masha—independent, confident, and demanding—intrigues Nigel with her defiance and complexity. She is not easily controlled or molded and refuses to be passively molded into a submissive role. Her autonomy and sometimes heartless boldness give her a magnetic pull that keeps Nigel in constant anticipation and desire. Their relationship is marked by passion and an intensity that is thrilling but sometimes painful. Though volatile and manipulative, she captivates him in ways he can't shake, even as her choices turn destructive.

Nigel's reaction to these two loves speaks volumes: while he tolerates and eventually moves away from the gentle, compliant Masha, he remains haunted and hurt by the impact of the fiery, unpredictable Masha. The tragic culmination of their love, her act of harming something he cherishes, symbolizes the ultimate break, a betrayal that goes beyond the personal and attacks his sense of loyalty and trust.

Ultimately, Nigel's journey with both women teaches the complexity of human relationships: the one who loves unconditionally may be taken for granted, while the one who challenges and defies can create an all-consuming passion. The story warns against mistaking self-sacrifice for love and suggests that in embracing one's own demands and authenticity—rather than suppressing them—people often find a love that truly respects them. True love will withstand, and perhaps even embrace, the contradictions, imperfections, and complexities that make us human.

Don't let a man doing small favors spark intense feelings within you. Be unapologetically yourself – be demanding, selfish, even a little mischievous. The one who truly loves you will embrace all of it, even the things that might irritate others.

Chapter 3

Relationship basics

The difference between someone who is "**playing**" versus someone genuinely invested often comes down to confidence, depth, and independence. When someone respects themselves, has their own boundaries, and approaches the relationship with a healthy balance of independence and openness, it signals authenticity. This often inspires a partner to step up, offer genuine respect, and invest in the relationship with equal sincerity.

In essence, real connection grows from mutual respect, curiosity, and the space to truly get to know each other over time.

How does a man distinguish between the one who plays it and the one who actually bought it?

We often hear of women who are kind, respectable, cultured, beautiful, and independent—yet struggle in relationships. While they embody many positive qualities, they sometimes display vulnerabilities that make them susceptible to manipulation. Some men sense these weaknesses and may play with their emotions or seek a more challenging partner.

Signs of Vulnerability:

- **Revealing Appearance:** If your attire is overly revealing, a man may see this as a lack of self-confidence, interpreting it as an attempt to seek validation. This often leads to him viewing you as an easy conquest, as you've left little to his imagination.
- **Oversharing:** Revealing too much about yourself too soon can give the impression of desperation. A man feels he doesn't need to invest effort to know you, as you've already laid everything out for him.
- **Immediate Availability:** If you're always free and responsive, he may see this as lack of personal depth, assuming you have no passions or pursuits outside of him, making the relationship feel unbalanced.
- **Agreeing to Everything:** Constantly aligning with his opinions, even against your own, suggests you lack boundaries. This can make you appear unassertive, which might eventually bore or repel him.

Signs of Self-Respect and Confidence:

- **Subtle Elegance in Dressing:** When you dress in a way that's feminine yet modest, you convey confidence. This tells a man you value more than just physical attraction.

- **Balanced Sharing:** Sharing personal details over time keeps him intrigued. He will want to understand you more deeply, valuing the mystery and recognizing your trust is earned, not freely given.
- **Independent Life:** Having hobbies, goals, and passions that don't center around him shows him that you are fulfilled and confident on your own. This independence attracts him, making him see you as a partner, not a dependent.
- **Respectful Dialogue:** Engaging in meaningful conversations and asserting your viewpoints reflects intellectual compatibility. He will respect and appreciate you for the substance you bring to the relationship.
- **Healthy Boundaries:** When you maintain boundaries and prioritize self-respect, he senses that you value yourself. This inspires him to value you equally, fearing to lose someone who respects herself.

In essence, a woman who values herself, embraces her independence, and expresses opinions will earn a man's respect. Such a woman doesn't chase or submit to superficial attractions but invites a genuine, lasting connection where both partners are valued equally.

In relationships, understanding what distinguishes someone genuine from someone merely "playing the game" can be complex, but it often boils down to a few key factors. Here's how these dynamics generally play out and the indicators that can help a man recognize a genuine connection versus something superficial:

Indicators of Superficial Attraction

1. **Over-reliance on Appearance:** When there's an overemphasis on dressing provocatively or being overly polished, it might signal insecurity. Often, when a man senses that someone is more focused on appearance than personality, he may perceive the relationship as shallow, as there's little left to his imagination or discovery.
2. **Oversharing Personal Information Early On:** Some individuals open up entirely too soon, sharing every intimate detail from the first conversation. While transparency is crucial, it's also important to build trust gradually. If someone reveals everything immediately, the other person may feel there's little left to discover or explore.
3. **Lack of Boundaries:** If a person is too eager to please and agrees with everything, even at the cost of their own preferences, it can be a red flag. Boundaries show self-respect and individuality; without them, a partner might see them as lacking depth or genuine self-worth.
4. **Constantly Available:** Being perpetually free or never having personal pursuits can make a

partner feel as if they aren't valued for who they are but rather as a time-filler. Relationships benefit when both individuals have personal goals and interests, as this adds richness and balance to the connection.

5. **Future Plans Too Soon:** Discussing marriage or hinting at a serious future early on can sometimes backfire. A man may interpret this as eagerness for the concept of a relationship rather than genuine interest in him as a person.
6. **Lack of Depth in Conversation:** Relationships thrive on meaningful exchanges. If a person keeps the dialogue superficial or lacks intellectual engagement, it often leaves a partner feeling as though there's no substantial connection beyond physical attraction.

Indicators of Genuine Connection and Interest

1. **Self-Confidence and Subtle Elegance:** Dressing with style rather than overt boldness often signals self-assurance. Confidence in one's personality, achievements, and values tends to be more attractive than a flashy appearance, inviting someone to appreciate deeper qualities.
2. **Balanced Disclosure:** Someone who reveals aspects of themselves slowly, over time, tends to cultivate more curiosity and respect. They might share their values, dreams, and history

gradually, allowing a man to feel like he's unwrapping a gift layer by layer.

3. **Personal Boundaries and Standards:** A person who isn't afraid to disagree, express personal opinions, or set boundaries demonstrates a strong sense of self. This often attracts genuine respect because it shows they have standards and are not simply looking for validation.
4. **Independent Interests and Goals:** A partner who has a full life of their own—personal goals, hobbies, and social connections—often attracts more respect and admiration. It's attractive to know someone doesn't rely entirely on a relationship for their happiness, making their time with a partner more meaningful.
5. **Natural Pace in Discussing the Future:** Someone who doesn't rush into discussions about marriage or a serious future often signals emotional maturity. They enjoy the process of getting to know their partner genuinely, giving the relationship a chance to evolve naturally. This often invites a man to step up and initiate deeper commitments on his own.
6. **Thoughtful, In-Depth Conversations:** A person who can engage deeply in conversations and share their thoughts meaningfully often fosters a sense of intellectual compatibility. This kind of

dialogue goes beyond surface attraction and helps build a relationship based on mutual respect and admiration.

7. **Strong Sense of Self and Value:** A partner who knows their worth, doesn't chase or cling, and is unafraid of being alone is often incredibly attractive. This kind of confidence signals that they are in the relationship by choice, not out of need, prompting a man to value them more.

The Power of Mutual Desire in Relationships

The foundation of a fulfilling relationship often rests on the mutual desire that partners feel for one another. While companionship, shared values, and emotional connection are essential for any lasting bond, desire brings a unique energy to a partnership. It fuels attraction, intimacy, and a sense of excitement that can deepen the connection between two people. When both partners genuinely desire each other, their relationship becomes a space where they feel valued, seen, and cherished, fostering a dynamic that enhances both emotional and physical intimacy. However, desire isn't merely about physical attraction; it's also a deep-rooted appreciation for each other's presence, qualities, and individuality.

For a relationship to thrive, this mutual desire must be nurtured continuously. Without it, even a seemingly stable partnership can start to feel stagnant or disconnected, as the lack of intimacy and longing often leads to frustration and emotional distance. On the other hand, when desire flows freely between partners, it brings joy and resilience to the relationship, making it easier to navigate challenges together. In the end, a healthy desire for one another isn't simply an element of romance—it's a vital force that strengthens the bond between partners and contributes to a meaningful, enduring connection.

Many women face challenges in choosing a life partner for various reasons, often overlooking a crucial element needed for a healthy, fulfilling, and lasting marriage: genuine mutual desire. This desire extends beyond companionship or attraction; it forms the foundation of a relationship built on understanding, affection, and companionship that feels natural and effortless. When intimacy is driven by deep, shared feelings rather than obligation, relationship challenges become easier to navigate and resolve. Trusting your choice wholeheartedly—free from societal pressure, fear of being left behind, or expectations around having children—is essential. Ultimately, the impact of a mismatched or unfulfilled relationship often falls on children, who bear the consequences.

Consider the story of Dima, a young woman known for her self-respect and integrity, who crossed paths with Joseph, an ambitious man with a stable, successful career. For years, Joseph's relationships had been based mostly on appearance, prioritizing superficial attraction over genuine compatibility. But when he met Dima, something shifted. Unlike anyone he had dated before, she captivated him with her self-assuredness, dignity, smile and warm sense of humor—qualities he rarely encountered.

Initially, Joseph couldn't fully understand why Dima had such an effect on him. Over time, he found himself not only drawn to her physical presence but increasingly to her character and values. She wasn't trying to impress him; instead, she brought honesty, intelligence, and a lighthearted humor to their conversations. For the first time, he felt a deep, genuine desire to be with someone, not because of societal expectations or appearances, but because of a true connection.

Through their growing relationship, Joseph realized he had been missing something essential in his life: an authentic partnership built on mutual respect and shared values. Dima's presence challenged his views on relationships and prompted him to reflect on his own desires. She had a grounding effect on him, making him question the life he wanted and the kind of man he aspired to be. No longer seeking temporary satisfaction, he now desired a lasting partnership with someone who made him feel seen and valued.

Dima, too, felt this connection. She recognized in Joseph a kind heart and a willingness to grow, despite his ambitious nature. She didn't feel the need to change herself to meet his expectations, nor did she feel pressured to settle for anything less than a partner who valued her fully. Their relationship developed slowly, with each discovering that true companionship is built on acceptance, patience, and an enduring respect for each other's individuality.

Their story highlights an essential lesson: a fulfilling relationship isn't built on superficial connections or external pressures but on a deep, genuine desire that fosters growth and support. Relationships grounded in mutual respect and affection create a safe space for both partners to grow, facing challenges together rather than as individuals bearing separate burdens.

For anyone seeking a lasting connection, it's essential to ask, "**Do I feel genuine desire and respect for this person?**" and "**Do we have shared values and goals that align with the future we both envision?"** Choosing a life partner is one of life's most significant decisions, so it's worth taking the time to understand what you genuinely need and want in a relationship.

In the end, trust in your choice wholeheartedly—not out of societal pressure, fear of being alone, or others' expectations, but because you feel fulfilled, valued, and genuinely seen by your partner. This depth of connection lays the foundation for a marriage that not only endures but thrives. And for those who may have children, this strong foundation sets a positive example, creating a legacy of love and respect for them to carry forward.

This is why Joseph saw Dima differently. He loved her qualities, but he neglected to appreciate her physical presence, forgetting his desire for her. He lacked a balance in his choices. Perhaps Dima, too, thought only rationally, overlooking her desire, simply saying, "**I love his love for me.**" She loved how he cared for her, his generosity, and his unwavering support whenever she needed him.

Girls, some advice: it's not wrong to choose a person who possesses all the qualities you want, whom you enjoy being with, and who fulfills your desire. Don't underestimate desire; it's a cornerstone of marriage. The real mistake is staying silent, enduring dissatisfaction, and wronging both yourself and your partner. Seek a man who embodies all the beautiful qualities and with whom you share a chemistry and harmony that's hard to explain. True chemistry is a shared attraction from both sides, not one-sided. Some say a woman's priority is only support, as if a relationship should be one-sided. This is misguided. Chemistry is a mutual connection, and without it, the relationship lacks essential depth, often leading to betrayal or unfulfilled longing.

Returning to Joseph and Dima, they made a rational choice, believing that shared qualities alone would make them compatible. After their honeymoon, reality hit hard. Living together was challenging, with feelings absent from their relationship. For them, intimacy became a mere duty as husband and wife. Dima often pretended to be asleep or tired, while for Joseph, intimacy was simply a way of fulfilling a biological need.

Both regretted their decision to be with each other, realizing they had overlooked the importance of sexual desire. Many people, especially some women, regard this as secondary, merely to satisfy a partner's needs or as a means for procreation. But desire is what makes us human, setting us apart from mere instinct. The desire for a specific person brings meaning beyond the physical aspect—it's about connection, exclusivity, and feeling chosen.

Let's look at another example. Fatma was thrilled at the beginning of her marriage to Ramon, feeling a strong desire for him. But Afzal had married her mainly to please his family; she wasn't his choice, nor did he feel attraction or desire for her except as a means for having children. Fatma tried to discuss this, wanting to feel feminine and desired by her husband. His response was polite but painful, essentially evading her need for connection and intimacy.

Now, let's turn to a story that ended positively. Magda and Wafeek met during their school days, and there was an undeniable chemistry between them. Despite their flaws, their personalities complemented each other. After graduating, they couldn't bear the separation, and Wafeek proposed. Now, after three years of marriage, they still share the same spark. They chose each other with conviction in both mind and heart, fully understanding that their relationship was built on a foundation of desire, respect, and companionship.

Why is their relationship successful? Because their connection remains strong, as if they were still dating. They both make efforts to keep things fresh, with Magda going out of her way to ensure Wafeek feels valued and desired, never giving him a reason to stray. Their problems stem from loving each other too much, rather than from neglect or resentment.

In relationships like theirs, both partners feel fulfilled and seen. This depth of connection keeps the relationship healthy, ensuring that even during disagreements, there's a willingness to resolve issues for the sake of their shared happiness and connection. A relationship built on mutual desire, respect, and shared values has the strength to thrive, and it's a foundation worth pursuing.

Another story, Terrie and Dean: The Challenge of Mismatched Libidos. Terrie and Dean had a relationship that, on the surface, seemed perfect. They had been together for years, sharing a deep bond rooted in friendship, shared values, and a similar sense of humor. Both had great respect for each other and a close emotional connection. However, a persistent issue arose that neither could ignore: their mismatched libidos.

Dean had a strong desire for physical intimacy and often felt that it was a way to deepen their bond. Terrie, on the other hand, felt satisfied with occasional intimacy, viewing other aspects of their relationship as the core of their connection. Over time, this difference began to strain them. Dean felt unfulfilled and at times, even rejected, while Terrie grew frustrated by what she perceived as constant pressure to meet Dean's needs.

They tried to navigate this by having open conversations about their desires, but despite both their efforts, the issue persisted. Eventually, they sought couples therapy, which helped them understand that intimacy could be approached in more creative and flexible ways. By focusing on non-pressured, affectionate touch and finding different ways to express closeness, they began to build a bridge over their differences. While their libidos didn't completely align, they developed a mutual understanding that allowed them to prioritize both physical and emotional needs, helping them reach a satisfying middle ground.

Suzi and Akram: The Impact of Past Trauma. Suzi and Akram's story reflects a common but often overlooked issue in relationships: the impact of past trauma on intimacy. Suzi had endured difficult experiences in her past that left her with emotional scars, which made it challenging for her to fully open up to intimacy, even with someone she loved deeply. Akram, unaware of the root of her hesitation, initially interpreted her reluctance as a lack of attraction or interest. Over time, Akram began to feel confused and hurt, unsure why Suzi seemed distant. Despite his frustration, he valued their relationship too much to give up without trying to understand. When Suzi finally opened up to him about her past, Akram was shocked, but he responded with compassion, realizing that her hesitation wasn't about him but rather the emotional weight she carried.

They both agreed that healing required time, patience, and support. Suzi sought therapy to help her process her past, and Akram actively participated by creating a safe, pressure-free environment for her. They worked together on emotional closeness first, understanding that rebuilding trust and healing from trauma would take time. With Akram's support, Suzi gradually felt comfortable, and their intimacy improved naturally as she healed. Their story illustrates the importance of understanding, empathy, and patience when past trauma affects a relationship.

Manal and Mohamed: The Absence of Desire and Emotional Disconnect

Manal and Mohamed had been married for a few years, and while they were committed to each other, they gradually fell into a routine that left little space for romance or connection. Their intimacy began to feel transactional, more out of obligation than genuine desire. For Manal, who had always been driven by an emotional connection, this lack of closeness became a source of deep dissatisfaction. Mohamed, who was focused on work and daily routines, didn't see the problem initially, believing that their marriage was stable because they had no visible conflict.

However, Manal started feeling invisible and began to withdraw emotionally. She realized that her desire for Mohamed had faded, replaced by a sense of duty and detachment. Mohamed, meanwhile, couldn't understand why she seemed distant and unenthusiastic, which created frustration on both sides. Manal knew they needed a change, and after some difficult conversations, she expressed her need for a deeper emotional bond.

Together, they began making an effort to reconnect by setting aside time each week to talk openly about their feelings, rediscover shared interests, and prioritize moments of affection without any specific expectations for physical intimacy. Gradually, their emotional connection began to rebuild, reigniting Manal's desire for Mohamed. Through mutual effort, they found that the renewed emotional intimacy fostered a natural physical closeness, reviving the passion they once shared. Their story highlights how emotional disconnect can lead to the loss of desire and how prioritizing emotional reconnection can restore intimacy.

Yasmine: Childhood Trauma and Desire for Revenge

Yasmine grew up in a home where she was supposed to feel safe, but her father's abuse shattered that sense of security. From a young age, she endured traumatic experiences that left deep scars, affecting her perception of men and intimacy. The betrayal from someone she trusted instilled in her a profound distrust of men. As she grew older, Yasmine felt an intense need to protect herself from vulnerability and even harbored feelings of anger and resentment.

Her trauma developed into a desire for revenge, not against any specific man, but as a shield to ensure she never felt helpless again. Despite meeting kind, supportive men who genuinely cared for her, Yasmine struggled to form connections, often sabotaging relationships out of fear and distrust. She found solace in therapy, where she could begin to process her pain and work toward reclaiming control over her life. Through a long and difficult healing journey, Yasmine learned that recovery would require patience and self-compassion. Gradually, she started to open herself up to the possibility of love, realizing that her past did not have to dictate her future.

Nisren and Amir: Forced Marriage and a Life of Emotional Turmoil

Nisren's life took a tragic turn when she was assaulted by a man named Amir, and her family forced her to marry him to "save her reputation." This forced marriage became a prison for her, trapping her in a constant cycle of emotional and psychological torment. Amir's controlling nature made the household tense and oppressive, and Nisren struggled with resentment and a deep sense of betrayal—not only by Amir but by her family for making her marry him.

With children to care for, Nisren felt even more trapped. Her protective instincts toward her children became extreme; she felt a need to shield them from the pain she had endured. However, her overprotectiveness created a stifling environment, where the children felt constantly monitored and restricted, leading to further tension in the household. Nisren's inability to process her trauma turned her home into a place of fear rather than comfort. Over time, she recognized the need for help, realizing that therapy could help her release some of her fears and guide her toward healthier ways to parent. Slowly, she began the difficult journey toward healing, not just for herself but for her children as well.

Healy and Her Husband: Struggling with Intimacy and Health Challenges

Healy had always been an open and expressive person, deeply enjoying the physical side of her relationship with her husband. But after he was diagnosed with a health condition that affected his ability to perform sexually, their intimacy faced a new challenge. Healy tried to be patient and supportive, understanding that his health was beyond his control, yet she couldn't ignore her own needs and feelings of frustration.
Her husband, feeling guilt and insecurity over his inability to meet her needs, started to withdraw emotionally, which only widened the distance between them. This lack of physical intimacy left Healy feeling neglected, and her attempts to discuss her needs often led to arguments, with her husband feeling inadequate and defensive. In a moment of vulnerability, Healy suggested exploring alternative ways to maintain intimacy, emphasizing that closeness wasn't solely about physical performance.

They both agreed to consult a therapist who specialized in intimacy and relationships affected by health issues. Through therapy, they found ways to reconnect emotionally and physically in ways that suited both their needs. By focusing on affection and closeness beyond traditional intimacy, they learned to keep their bond strong despite the challenges. Healy's story reflects how open communication, compassion, and willingness to adapt can help couples navigate intimacy issues stemming from health problems.

Veronica and Nader: The Impact of War and Mental Health Struggles.

Veronica and Nader's relationship was shaped by their shared experiences of war. Both had lived through trauma, displacement, and loss, which left deep emotional scars. While they had initially bonded over their shared experiences, the unresolved trauma from those years of conflict began to take a toll on their relationship. Nader, who struggled with PTSD, would often have flashbacks and bouts of intense anger or withdrawal, leaving Veronica feeling helpless and isolated.

Veronica, too, was haunted by her past, experiencing nightmares and bouts of anxiety that made it difficult for her to fully engage with life or with Nader. Their relationship became strained as they each grappled with mental health issues they couldn't always understand or control. The intimacy between them faded, replaced by emotional distance and the heavy weight of unspoken pain.

In time, Veronica realized that their survival depended on seeking help. She encouraged Nader to attend therapy sessions together, where they could confront their trauma with the support of professionals who understood the impacts of war. With time, patience, and therapy, they began to reconnect, finding comfort in mutual understanding. Their story highlights the importance of addressing mental health and trauma to rebuild intimacy and trust, showing that even the most devastating experiences don't have to define the future of a relationship.

Each of these examples delves into complex situations that illustrate how trauma, health issues, look and extreme circumstances like war can impact intimacy, communication, and the overall health of relationships. These stories emphasize the need for understanding, compassion, and a willingness to seek help to overcome such deeply rooted challenges.

Ladies, here's some advice! It's perfectly okay to choose someone who meets all your criteria, someone you know you'll enjoy being with and who will fulfill your desires. Don't underestimate the importance of desire—it's essential in any relationship. The mistake is staying silent, tolerating an unfulfilling relationship, and ultimately doing a disservice to both yourself and your partner.

Look for a man who not only has the qualities you admire but also shares that inexplicable chemistry and harmony with you—something that doesn't need explaining. Chemistry is about mutual attraction, not just a one-sided feeling. Don't let anyone tell you that support alone should be your top priority. It's more than that; a deep connection goes beyond just being "there" for each other. Being with a partner you lack chemistry with can feel empty and forced, and, truthfully, that lack of spark is often what leads to discontent and even betrayal. Seek a relationship with both mutual respect and undeniable attraction, because true chemistry is the foundation of lasting happiness.

Friends, my dears...

A word of advice, girls: never abandon your friends.

Men understand this naturally, but too often, women pull away from friendships when they get into serious relationships. It's a shame, especially if those friendships are genuine, close, and dear to your heart. Don't let the warmth of a romantic relationship blind you to the importance of having a strong circle of friends. That "light of your eyes" might fade, but true friendships endure.

Ladies, if your friends are meaningful to you—people you love and who love you—why let them drift away once you're in a relationship? Many men respect and value a partner with her own life, friends, and interests. A woman who is fulfilled by her friendships, hobbies, and passions doesn't rely solely on her partner for happiness, and that independence only enhances the relationship. Ideally, life is a balance: 50% for him and 50% for the other parts of your life, including your friends.

Unfortunately, this understanding is often ignored, and many think that a woman's life should revolve entirely around her partner. But here's the truth: a man respects a woman who has a second life, one that doesn't revolve solely around him. When he sees you fulfilled by friendships, hobbies, and things you love, he will start to value your time and the moments you share.

Girls, let's be real—how many times have we heard stories of women who dropped everything for a man, only to end up feeling abandoned or left on the sidelines when he returned to his interests and friends? Here's the difference between a woman who maintains her friendships while in a relationship and one who sacrifices everything for her partner:

Without her friends:

- Her happiness depends entirely on him.
- She's constantly available, leaving little room for her own interests or friends.
- He feels no challenge and may start to take her for granted, knowing he can have her attention whenever he wants.

With her friends:

- She's full of energy, confidence, and joy, fueled by the support of a close circle.
- She is fulfilled and engaged with her own interests, friendships, and activities, making her partner value her time.
- He sees her time as precious and is motivated to be a part of her happiness, wanting to "steal" moments with her because she's not constantly available.
- There's natural dialogue and excitement between them, as she brings something new back to the relationship after seeing friends and living her life.

A man admires a woman who is her own person, whose happiness doesn't depend solely on him. This mystery and independence create a spark and keep him engaged, wondering what she's up to and eager to share in her life.

The bottom line? Keep your friendships close, keep your life rich with meaning, and your partner will respect you for it. Instead of being taken for granted, you'll be his main focus, someone he cherishes because you bring genuine energy and balance to the relationship.

Take Care of Your Appearance, My Dear

Far too often, I've seen girls fall into the trap of neglecting their appearance, health, and well-being once they settle into a stable relationship. This is one of the biggest mistakes! Taking care of yourself isn't just about beauty—it's about self-respect and confidence. In the beginning, attraction often centers on physical appearance, but as a relationship deepens, personality takes center stage. That doesn't mean you should stop taking pride in how you present yourself.

Your appearance is a powerful tool. When you look after yourself, you're not only boosting your own confidence but also making a lasting impression on him. It's not about being perfectly groomed 24/7, but about maintaining cleanliness, eating well, and caring for your skin and body. Makeup, high heels, and fancy outfits aren't the measure—self-care is. Men may say that "it's what's on the inside that counts" or that "looks fade," but don't be fooled; if you take care of both the inside and outside, he'll be captivated.

Self-care equals confidence, which fuels his admiration and even jealousy, keeping the spark alive. This kind of love is timeless. A woman who prioritizes her health and well-being isn't just seen as beautiful but as someone with purpose and strength. Men respect and admire a partner who values herself independently of him.

Too often, I see women start to invest in their appearance just to "secure" a man, only to let that interest fade once they're in a stable relationship. There is no such thing as a "guarantee" in relationships! A woman who stops taking care of herself may inadvertently signal to her partner that her efforts were only about winning him over. Over time, this can erode his interest and, worse, diminish the level of admiration and even jealousy he feels. If he no longer feels that subtle jealousy, you may find yourself wondering why—and it often stems from this lack of personal care. Men are naturally inclined to notice the small details about a woman's appearance—her clothing, her hair, even her nail polish. Embrace this knowledge. Taking care of yourself is not about vanity but about nurturing your greatest asset: yourself.

Self-Care from the Inside Out

While many girls look stunning on the outside, they often overlook the importance of "**internal care**." Just as there's external beauty, there's internal beauty too. Taking care of yourself doesn't mean a dramatic change like plastic surgery.

Instead, it's about making self-care a daily habit. It's a lifelong commitment that pays off as you grow older and can be achieved in small, consistent steps:

Healthy Eating

Eating well is a cornerstone of self-care. Avoid crash diets and extreme restrictions—health should be a lifestyle, not a temporary fix. Drink plenty of water, aim for at least one protein-rich meal a day, and limit sugary drinks. Remember, your body is your temple, and treating it well reflects in every aspect of your life.

Daily Movement

Just a few minutes of activity each day can have a powerful long-term impact. Exercise doesn't have to be limited to the gym; it can be as simple as cleaning your room, watering plants, or running errands. There's always time if you make it a priority. Avoid excuses—make movement part of your daily life, and your energy will reflect it.

Personal Grooming

Some girls are naturally blessed with great hair, flawless skin, or beautiful nails, but it's essential to maintain these traits. Cleanliness and self-care are crucial. Develop a simple skincare routine to keep your skin radiant and youthful.

Moisturize daily, both your face and body. Regular self-care rituals go a long way in keeping you feeling fresh and confident.

Emotional Balance and Confidence

We often hear that women are more emotional than men, but this belief doesn't tell the whole story. Women are simply more open about their emotions, whereas men are often taught to hide theirs. Here's a truth many overlook: men are drawn to women who can control their emotions while still being genuine. When a woman is self-assured and not constantly afraid of losing him, he feels the urge to stay close and connected to her, feeling that he can never fully "guarantee" her.

Men dislike extremes. They aren't drawn to partners who are overly emotional, but they also don't connect well with someone entirely rational and unfeeling. Balance is key. Men, too, experience strong emotions but often keep them hidden. For a woman, talking to friends and family can help her process feelings, while men may prefer to keep these things to themselves. This difference means that men can seem distant or unaffected by a breakup or conflict, but over time, they feel the absence deeply, often long after a woman has moved on.

A man may initially act as though he's unbothered, but the reality is different. He might spend time with others, even appear to move on, but eventually, he'll feel the void left by someone significant. This internal struggle and delayed response are natural for men, while women tend to be more expressive and straightforward. Both approaches have their strengths, but understanding these dynamics can help women see why it's essential to maintain their confidence and independence. Ultimately, caring for yourself—inside and out—is an expression of self-love that resonates in every part of your life, especially in your relationships. When you treat yourself as a priority, you naturally become a woman who is valued, admired, and never taken for granted.

Additional Advice for Self-Care and Confidence

Along with self-care, hygiene and choosing a style that truly suits you are essential for building confidence and enhancing intimacy. Taking care of yourself doesn't have to mean following every trend or overspending. True confidence and allure come from authenticity, cleanliness, and knowing what works for you.

1. Prioritize Personal Hygiene as Part of Self-Care

Hygiene is a foundational part of self-respect and confidence. It's not just about appearance but about feeling good in your own skin, which enhances every area of life, including intimacy. That's why I created Duchess Prestige, a cosmetic line dedicated to achieving flawless skin and prioritizing full-body hygiene for a smooth, beautifully scented experience. Our signature products—body shower scrub, body lotion, and face cleanser—are designed to leave you with a soft, fresh, and irresistible fragrance, so you feel confident and radiant every day. Good hygiene shows that you value yourself and your body, and this attention to cleanliness naturally increases your confidence and comfort around others.

- **Daily Showering and Skincare Routine:** Start with a shower each day to feel refreshed and clean. Choose soaps and body washes that nourish your skin, and exfoliate weekly to keep your skin soft and glowing.
- **Oral Hygiene:** Don't underestimate the power of a fresh smile and clean breath. Brush and floss regularly, and consider using mouthwash for extra freshness. This routine helps with self-confidence and ensures you're comfortable in close interactions.
- **Hair and Nail Care:** Regularly washing and conditioning your hair keeps it healthy and shiny. Don't neglect your nails, either—keep them clean, trimmed, and moisturized, whether you prefer a polished look or a natural style.
- **Fragrance:** A subtle fragrance can boost your confidence and leave a lasting impression. Choose a scent that feels authentic to you rather than what's popular, and make it a part of your daily routine.That's why I choose to use my own Duchess Prestige perfumes, Heavenly and Life. These fragrances are crafted to evoke confidence and elegance,

creating an unforgettable aura that lingers beautifully. Each scent is a blend of sophistication and allure, designed to make every day feel extraordinary.

2. Wear What Suits You, Not Just What's Trending

While it's easy to be influenced by the latest trends, confidence comes from wearing clothes that flatter your body type, make you feel good, and align with your personality. Fashion changes constantly, but true style is timeless.

- **Choose Clothes that Enhance Your Shape:** Find styles that highlight your unique features and make you feel comfortable. You'll feel more confident when you're not trying to fit into a trend that doesn't suit your natural look or body type.
- **Invest in Quality over Quantity:** You don't need to overspend to look your best. Focus on a few quality items that you love and that make you feel fabulous, rather than buying multiple pieces you may rarely wear.
- **Define Your Own Style:** Personal style is powerful. Take time to figure out what colors, cuts, and fabrics work best for you. When you wear clothes that resonate with who you are, you naturally feel more confident.

3. Budget Smartly and Spend Wisely

True self-care doesn't require spending beyond your means. Instead, focus on sustainable habits that keep you feeling great without straining your budget. Financial responsibility is part of self-care, allowing you to invest in things that truly matter.

- **Set a Budget for Self-Care:** Allocate a realistic amount for skincare, clothes, and personal needs. Avoid overspending on products or treatments that don't align with your core needs.
- **DIY Self-Care Routines:** Many effective skincare and hygiene routines can be done at home. Find natural, affordable alternatives for expensive beauty treatments, such as homemade face masks, natural oils, and at-home manicures.

4. Hygiene as the Key to Confidence in Intimacy

Good hygiene is essential for sexual confidence and comfort. Feeling clean, fresh, and comfortable in your own skin builds trust and confidence with your partner, making intimacy a more natural, enjoyable experience.

- **Routine Freshness:** Cleanse yourself before intimacy with gentle, unscented products that maintain your skin's natural balance. Good personal hygiene shows respect for yourself and your partner.

- **Wear Clean, Comfortable Clothing:** Opt for breathable fabrics that keep you feeling fresh throughout the day. Regularly changing into clean clothes helps you feel your best, even during casual, relaxed moments.
- **Embrace Self-Care as a Routine:** When you view hygiene as an act of self-love and confidence, it becomes more than a routine—it's an affirmation of your worth. This self-assurance translates to a natural confidence that enhances both emotional and physical intimacy.

In essence, personal hygiene and self-care go hand in hand with confidence. By focusing on cleanliness, choosing a style that truly suits you, and spending within your means, you create a foundation of self-respect that radiates in every interaction. When you care for yourself in ways that feel authentic and genuine, you're not only more attractive to others but also deeply empowered in your own skin.

The Plan:

Constructive advice for fostering healthy emotional dynamics in relationships. It emphasizes individuality, emotional balance, and respect as keys to strong, lasting connections.

This is an extensive piece examining gender dynamics in relationships, particularly focusing on how men and women often approach emotions differently. key points:

Understanding Relationship Dynamics and Emotional Balance

In relationships, men and women often navigate emotions differently due to biological, social, and psychological factors. Traditionally, men are seen as managing emotions with a higher degree of restraint, while women are often perceived as more expressive with their feelings. However, achieving a balance is critical to maintaining a stable, healthy relationship.

Emotional Dynamics in Relationships:

1. **Emotional Control and Balance:** Men may find it easier to compartmentalize emotions and focus on rational problem-solving in stressful situations, which can sometimes give them an advantage in maintaining perspective. Conversely, women often express their emotions more freely and can feel deeply connected to their partner. However, unchecked emotions may sometimes lead to stress within the relationship.
2. **Misunderstandings and Emotional Responses:** Misunderstandings are common, but it's how each partner responds that shapes

the relationship. For instance, if one partner becomes overly sensitive to perceived changes in the other's behavior, it can lead to insecurity and conflict. Observing without assuming negative intent can help both partners respond thoughtfully instead of reactively.

3. **Managing Expectations and Communication:** Women may sometimes feel pressured to cater to their partner's needs excessively, which can lead to an imbalance in the relationship. It's essential to maintain individuality and not lose oneself in the relationship by setting healthy boundaries. Clear communication helps avoid the expectation that one partner should fulfill every emotional need of the other.
4. **Respect for Individuality:** Authenticity matters. When entering a relationship, showing genuine qualities rather than projecting a façade of extreme strength or emotional resilience can foster trust. Men generally appreciate emotional stability but also value a partner who respects their independence and individuality. Over time, allowing space for mystery and curiosity can sustain interest and encourage deeper connections.
5. **Self-Confidence and Healthy Boundaries**: A confident partner knows their worth, respects themselves, and doesn't compromise personal values for the sake of the relationship.

This approach creates a foundation of mutual respect. Avoid bending over backward to please your partner or conform to their expectations if it means sacrificing your identity or comfort.

6. **Embracing Mystery Without Hidden Agendas:** Mystery can be an appealing trait, as it keeps a relationship dynamic and intriguing. However, mystery should not be confused with secrecy or deceit. Instead, it's about maintaining a sense of independence and personal interest outside the relationship, which can prevent complacency and keep things exciting.
7. **Financial Independence and Mutual Support:** It's important to foster financial equality and independence in a relationship. When both partners contribute and respect each other's financial autonomy, it prevents one partner from feeling overly dependent or controlled, which supports a balanced partnership.

Ultimately, the success of a relationship depends on how well both partners understand, respect, and balance each other's emotional needs. Authenticity, clear boundaries, and self-confidence are crucial. Building a relationship based on mutual respect, shared values, and emotional maturity can lead to a lasting and fulfilling partnership.

Understanding Emotional Differences in Relationships

Men and women often approach emotions differently in relationships. Generally, men have a greater tendency to manage or restrain their emotions in social settings, influenced by how they are perceived by others. Women, by contrast, may openly express their emotions, even over seemingly minor issues, which can sometimes add stress to a relationship.

Women often invest deeply when they love someone, which can make them more vulnerable to emotional exhaustion. This level of emotional involvement sometimes leaves them feeling unappreciated if they sense a lack of reciprocation. However, if a woman remains less emotionally attached to someone who adores her, this can create a different dynamic. Her emotional distance might paradoxically increase the man's desire to be with her, as he feels the need to earn her attention and affection.

A common challenge arises when a woman expects a man to remain perpetually attentive and emotionally present. However, a man's engagement often fluctuates, especially as he balances other aspects of his life. If women can resist the urge to overanalyze or question a perceived change in attention, they may notice that men naturally return to the relationship without needing reminders of their partner's expectations.

Balancing Emotional Expression

Men and women typically rely on different levels of intuition, emotion, and rationality in decision-making.

Men, on average, might use:

- 70% rationality
- 26% emotions
- 4% intuition

Women may rely more on:

- 70% emotions
- 23% intuition
- 7% rationality

This difference in emotional makeup can lead to misunderstandings. Men may find it easier to "let go" of conflicts with friends, quickly moving past issues, whereas women might dwell on disagreements, feeling deeply hurt or revisiting old arguments.

Tips for Reducing Relationship Strain

1. **Observe His Behavior:** Instead of directly questioning changes in behavior, quietly note patterns and consider discussing feelings with a trusted friend for perspective.

2. **Avoid Emotional Outbursts:** If upset, take a moment before reacting. Write down feelings but wait an hour before deciding to share them. This pause often reveals whether the reaction was immediate or part of a more significant issue.
3. **Maintain Some Mystery:** Avoid disclosing too much too quickly in the relationship. This keeps a man intrigued, while still allowing him to gradually understand your deeper self over time.

Playing the Long Game in Relationships

It's natural for many women to present a strong, independent persona initially, but maintaining this balance is key. Men often seek partners who are both resilient and feminine. Confidence, calmness, and independence are attractive, but letting a man feel he is needed can foster balance.

Ultimately, a successful relationship is about being genuine while understanding that both men and women have unique emotional needs and responses. Recognizing and respecting these differences can lead to a more fulfilling and harmonious connection.

Two examples to illustrate the dynamics discussed:

Example 1: Nabila & Mohamed

Scenario: Nabila and Mohamed have been in a relationship for two years. Nabila is caring and expressive, often sharing her feelings with Mohamed. She loves Mohamed deeply and often wonders if he feels the same way, especially on days when he seems distant or doesn't respond to her messages as quickly.

Situation: One weekend, Mohamed tells Nabila he wants to go camping with his friends. Although she knows he's passionate about spending time outdoors, she feels a bit hurt. She worries he might prefer his friends' company over hers and starts overthinking the situation. She texts him, "I feel like you're pulling away from me." Mohamed, who sees this as just a weekend away, gets frustrated and doesn't know how to reassure her without feeling trapped.

Outcome: Instead of sending that text, Nabila takes a moment to think about Mohamed's feelings and recognizes that she's just nervous about being apart for the weekend. She reaches out to a friend instead and decides to plan something for herself. The weekend goes by, and when Mohamed returns, he surprises her with stories from his trip and a renewed enthusiasm to spend time with her. By giving him space and not letting her initial emotional reaction drive her response, Nabila strengthens their relationship without creating unnecessary tension.

Example 2: Christopher & Natalia

Scenario: Christopher and Natalia have been dating for a few months. Natalia is very ambitious and independent, which is part of what initially attracted Christopher to her. She maintains her own life, hobbies, and friendships, and Christopher admires her confidence. However, as they get closer, Natalia starts feeling that Christopher doesn't always pay her the attention she'd like, especially when he's busy with work.

Situation: One evening, Christopher gets caught up in a project and forgets to text Natalia back for hours. Instead of asking him directly if he's upset or if he still cares, Natalia chooses not to take his silence personally. She keeps herself busy with her own plans, knowing he'll reach out when he's able.

Outcome: Later that night, Christopher finishes his project and calls Natalia, relieved she didn't get upset over his delay. He says, "Thanks for being understanding; I was swamped, but I've been looking forward to talking to you." This response reassures Natalia that her decision to give him space paid off. By maintaining her independence and not pushing him for constant attention, Natalia keeps Christopher engaged and reinforces the healthy balance in their relationship.

In both examples, Nabila and Natalia manage their emotional responses by giving space and recognizing that both partners need time and freedom to express themselves.

This approach can lead to greater mutual respect, trust, and appreciation in a relationship.

Valuing Yourself: The Importance of Emotional and Physical Boundaries in New Relationships

A comprehensive look at the concept of valuing one's body and emotions and how holding off on physical intimacy at the start of a relationship can strengthen it and protect someone from unnecessary heartbreak.

Entering a new relationship often brings excitement, curiosity, and the hope of a strong emotional connection. In the early stages, it's easy to feel swept away by chemistry or pressure, but this is also a critical time to establish boundaries and affirm your values. Respecting your own emotional and physical boundaries—especially by not rushing into physical intimacy—can set the foundation for a healthy, lasting relationship. Here's why it's important to approach physical intimacy thoughtfully, how it shapes men's perceptions, and how it ultimately influences the direction of a relationship.

1. Understanding Your Value

One of the most empowering mindsets in any new relationship is understanding that your body and emotions are valuable. This isn't just about physical attraction or how you look; it's about the totality of who you are—your mind, heart, and spirit. Each of us is unique, with individual experiences, beliefs, and dreams, making us much more than just a physical being. Recognizing this inherent worth gives you the strength to choose only those who genuinely appreciate you beyond the surface.

When you set boundaries and take time to build trust and genuine connection before engaging physically, you communicate that you value yourself and expect others to do the same. This sets a standard, letting the other person know that you're serious about the kind of relationship you want and that you aren't simply looking for superficial validation or fleeting connection.

2. How Men Perceive Boundaries and Restraint

Men, especially those looking for long-term relationships, generally appreciate and respect boundaries, even if they don't always express it. When a woman sets boundaries around intimacy early on, it sends a clear message: she respects herself and expects the same from her partner. This can be especially powerful because it challenges common assumptions and stereotypes about physical relationships.

For men, the experience of building a relationship without rushing physical intimacy often leads to a stronger emotional connection. Many men appreciate when a woman values herself enough to take time to know him first, as this gives him the chance to see her for who she is, not just the immediate physical attraction. Additionally, by not rushing into intimacy, he has the chance to prove that his interest is not only about physical desires but also about understanding her on a deeper level. This can help the relationship start on a foundation of genuine connection rather than one clouded by physical expectations.

However, there are men who may react negatively if they sense that intimacy isn't happening as quickly as they want. These are typically men who may not be ready for commitment or who are primarily interested in a short-term connection. While this may feel discouraging, it's actually a blessing in disguise. By establishing and maintaining your boundaries, you allow those who aren't genuinely interested in you to move on—ultimately saving you from potential hurt and emotional drain.

3. Example of Hanouf and Faisal to further illustrate the impact of pacing a relationship.

Let's take a look at Hanouf and Faisal to see how these dynamics play out in real life.

Scenario: Hanouf and Faisal meet at a friend's gathering and immediately feel a connection. They start talking, and over a few weeks, Faisal makes it clear that he's interested in getting to know her better. They go on several dates, and Faisal seems attentive and charming, always complimenting Hanouf and showing her affection.

However, after a month of dating, Faisal begins to drop hints about taking their relationship to a physical level. Hanouf, although attracted to him, feels it's too soon and wants to continue building trust and emotional closeness before moving forward physically. She's had experiences in the past where she rushed intimacy and later regretted it, so this time, she's determined to go slowly and ensure Faisal is interested in her for the right reasons.

Outcome: Faisal initially seems to understand and even admire Hanouf's decision. But after another month, he starts expressing frustration, questioning why she isn't ready to take the next step. He even suggests that maybe she isn't as interested in him as he thought, making her feel pressured and guilty. Hanouf stands her ground, calmly explaining that she values her emotions and body and wants to be sure their connection is genuine.

This response gives Faisal two options: respect her decision and show he's committed, or move on if his main goal was physical intimacy. Faisal, realizing he's more interested in a physical relationship than a committed one, begins pulling away. Though hurt, Hanouf understands that she made the right choice in holding her boundaries. She avoided investing deeply in someone whose intentions were not aligned with her own.

In this example, Hanouf's decision to prioritize her emotional and physical well-being helped her see Faisal's true intentions. By valuing herself and being clear about her boundaries, she avoided prolonging a relationship that might have led to heartbreak.

4. Why Rushing Intimacy Can Harm a Relationship

When a relationship becomes physical too quickly, it can cloud judgment and mask potential red flags. Physical intimacy often releases powerful emotions, making it easy to ignore or overlook issues that might otherwise be concerning. For instance, someone may overlook incompatibility, lack of shared values, or mismatched life goals if they feel bonded through physical closeness.

Taking time before engaging in intimacy allows each person to assess the relationship more objectively. It enables both partners to build a foundation of trust, communication, and emotional closeness—elements that are essential for a long-term relationship. When intimacy is delayed, both partners have a chance to prove their interest, intentions, and commitment without being influenced by physical attachment.

5. Developing Emotional Resilience and Confidence

Holding off on intimacy can be challenging, especially if there is strong chemistry. But maintaining this boundary requires emotional resilience and self-confidence. Knowing that your emotions are valuable and that not everyone deserves access to your most vulnerable self is empowering.

By maintaining this perspective, you avoid the trap of seeking validation through physical intimacy or rushing into something just because it feels good at the moment.

If someone genuinely cares, they will respect your choice and understand that waiting is part of building something lasting. On the other hand, if someone loses interest because intimacy isn't immediate, it's a clear sign that their commitment was shallow. This knowledge helps you navigate relationships more confidently, understanding that the right person will appreciate your values rather than pressure you to compromise.

6. Tips for Building a Relationship Slowly and Intentionally

- **Communicate Openly:** Share your reasons for wanting to move slowly. This transparency can help your partner understand your perspective, reducing misunderstandings.
- **Stay Firm on Your Boundaries:** Once you've set a boundary, stick to it. Consistency in your decisions will demonstrate self-respect and ensure that your partner respects your boundaries as well.
- **Get to Know Each Other's Values:** Use this time to discuss life goals, values, and expectations for the future. These conversations can reveal compatibility on a deeper level, beyond physical attraction.

- **Observe How They React:** Pay attention to how your partner responds to your boundaries. Are they respectful and understanding, or do they pressure you? Their reaction is often a reflection of their intentions.
- **Stay Focused on Building Emotional Intimacy:** Instead of focusing on physical closeness, prioritize emotional intimacy. Take time to understand each other's pasts, dreams, and vulnerabilities.

In a society that often promotes fast-paced relationships, taking time to build trust and respect before engaging in physical intimacy can feel challenging but is ultimately rewarding. Valuing your emotions and body means prioritizing your well-being and ensuring that any relationship you enter is based on genuine connection and mutual respect.

By setting boundaries around intimacy, you protect yourself from emotional hurt and invite only those who respect and appreciate you fully. The right person will see your decision as a sign of strength and self-respect, not as a rejection. And remember, when someone's intentions are genuine, they'll be willing to wait and build a meaningful bond that respects both of your values.

Holding off on intimacy is not about playing games or withholding affection; it's about valuing yourself enough to only share that part of you with someone truly deserving. Hanouf's story with Faisal illustrates the importance of self-respect and the clarity that boundaries can bring. In the end, the right relationship is one that values who you are in all aspects, recognizing that true connection takes time to build.

Understanding Financial Compatibility and Valuing Yourself in Relationships

Financial compatibility plays a vital role in relationships. It's not about finding someone wealthy but about choosing a partner who is financially stable, ideally on the same level as you or better. Financial stability can significantly impact both partners' well-being and help prevent future challenges.

Ayesha's Story

Ayesha was a financially stable woman who started dating Khaled, a charming man who, while appealing in personality, was financially far less secure than she was. Despite her friends advising her, "Ayesha, money isn't everything, but if he's significantly less stable, it could become a real issue later," she was swept up in her emotions. She was convinced Khaled appreciated her support and loyalty.

Ignoring her friends' advice, Ayesha replied, "**I don't mind helping him. If he needs something, I'm here.**" But what Ayesha didn't realize was that Khaled had come to see her financial stability as his own security net. He stayed not out of love, but out of dependency.

Months later, Ayesha came back to her friends, devastated. **"I gave him everything, even during his worst times, and I suspect he used my support to impress someone else!"** When she confronted him, his response was blunt: **"This is me. Take it or leave it."**
Ayesha's story reveals why financial compatibility is important in relationships. It's not about money itself but about balance and mutual respect.

Lalee's Story

Lalee's experience offers a unique example of a financially imbalanced relationship that worked. Lalee, financially stable and independent, was dating Youssef, who had fewer financial resources. Early on, Youssef hinted that she should help cover their expenses. Lalee, however, remained grounded and set clear boundaries.

When Youssef mentioned that she could "help him out in a rough spot," she confidently replied, "I look forward to the day you invite me." Lalee's calm boundary surprised Youssef. He was used to partners who would spend on him without hesitation, but Lalee valued her own standards and respected his role in the relationship.

Youssef, initially uncomfortable, began to see things differently. Motivated by Lalee's stance, he started planning to contribute financially. Lalee didn't demand it; her confidence and self-worth inspired him to take responsibility. Over time, he found genuine satisfaction in providing for her, reshaping his view on both finances and his role in the relationship.

Lalee's story highlights how setting self-respecting boundaries can inspire respect and growth in a partner. By valuing herself, she encouraged Youssef to meet her standards, enriching their relationship.

Key Takeaways for Women: Valuing Yourself and Setting Financial Boundaries

These stories underscore the importance of self-respect, financial boundaries, and choosing partners with similar values. Ayesha's story warns against letting emotions cloud judgment, while Lalee's experience shows the value of respecting your worth.

In any relationship, remember:

- **Keep financial matters private initially** – Don't reveal too much about your financial situation early in the relationship.
- **Set clear boundaries** – Avoid letting financial issues affect your judgment or compromise your values.
- **Value your self-worth** – Your self-respect sets the tone for how a partner perceives their role and responsibilities.

Ultimately, financial stability in relationships isn't about who pays for what. It's about creating a balanced, respectful partnership rooted in shared values. When you hold onto your principles and self-worth, you're more likely to find a relationship that respects and fulfills you both emotionally and financially.

The Dream vs. The Ready House Analogy

Think of relationships as two types of houses:
A "**dream house**" that a partner builds with effort, versus a "**ready house**" they simply move into. If a man sees a woman as a "**dream house**," he values her deeply, having invested his time, care, and commitment. He respects her because he has worked to be with her. On the other hand, a "ready house" is easy to obtain and leave, lacking the same depth of value.

Lalee chose to be a "**dream house**" by setting high standards for herself, making Youssef realize her worth. Ayesha, unfortunately, was treated as a "**ready house,**" a resource without effort from Khaled. Which would you prefer to be?

Choose to value yourself. Stand strong in your principles, and you will attract someone who respects both you and the relationship.

Wrong use of technology: Embracing Old Values in Modern Times: A Lesson in Dignity and Privacy

In today's fast-paced world, technology has transformed the way we connect, share, and express ourselves. However, not everyone navigates this change wisely, especially when it comes to preserving personal values and dignity. In relationships, and particularly for women, this challenge becomes even more pronounced. Let's explore two perspectives through the story of an English couple, Emma and Jack, who approached the influence of technology and social trends in very different ways.

Emma's Story: A Commitment to Timeless Values

Emma valued her privacy and respected her sense of self. Though she enjoyed the benefits of technology, she was careful to protect her personal life. She believed that not everything had to be shared with the world. Her online presence was professional and purposeful, revealing little about her personal relationships or private life.

Emma's sense of mystery intrigued Jack. He admired her for staying grounded, valuing her dignity, and not letting trends dictate her principles. For Emma, her privacy was her strength; she believed that keeping some things private made her stand out. She didn't rush to show every detail of her life online, choosing instead to share selectively. Each step in her relationship with Jack was intentional, respecting both herself and him by taking things slowly.

Emma's approach created a sense of depth and respect in their relationship. Jack felt genuinely invested in getting to know her, and their connection deepened because he had to make an effort. Her mystery kept him curious and excited, proving that dignity and privacy can be powerful in a world where oversharing is the norm.

Sophie's Story: Chasing Trends at Cost of Self-Worth

Sophie, on the other hand, believed that staying trendy meant embracing everything modern, including sharing her life extensively on social media. From the first days of her relationship with James, she posted about every date, every moment, and every detail. Sophie's approach was to prove her worth by showing that she was always "in the know" and keeping up with the times.

But by making herself so accessible, Sophie unknowingly diluted her uniqueness. James felt like he knew everything about her within days, as her life was an open book online. There was no sense of mystery or depth, and soon, James began to lose interest. While Sophie thought that openness would draw him closer, it had the opposite effect. Her need to "keep up" had cost her the chance to create a meaningful bond, as James felt no need to discover more about her on his own.

Sophie's story is a reminder of the risk in abandoning personal principles for the sake of modern trends.

Technology should be a tool to enhance life, not expose every corner of it.

Lessons in Privacy, Dignity, and Respect in Relationships

The contrasting stories of Emma and Sophie highlight essential lessons:

- **Privacy Is a Powerful Asset:** Emma's selective sharing kept her relationship with Jack meaningful. She believed that giving everything away too soon robs a relationship of the natural excitement and respect that comes from taking time to truly know each other.
- **Dignity Over Trends:** Sophie's eagerness to "**keep up**" by sharing everything online only made her seem less intriguing. While it's tempting to follow social trends, real respect in a relationship comes from valuing oneself and not compromising dignity to fit in.
- **Use Technology with Purpose:** Technology should enhance your life, not expose it entirely. In the West, many people use platforms to share their talents or professional life while keeping their personal matters private. By separating personal from public life, they preserve relationships and avoid unnecessary complications.

- **Real Connection Takes Time:** Emma understood that relationships need time to grow naturally. By allowing Jack to discover her gradually, she built a foundation based on mutual effort and respect.

These stories encourage us to think critically about how we use technology and whether we let trends dictate our values. Real confidence comes from valuing yourself, maintaining your dignity, and knowing that genuine connections are built on respect and curiosity. Choose to be like Emma, who uses technology wisely, preserves her mystery, and embraces the beauty of timeless principles

Embracing Confidence and Self-Respect in Relationships

In relationships, confidence and self-respect are key. Sometimes, people make the mistake of becoming overly invested in someone who doesn't reciprocate their feelings, while those they're less interested in seem to cling to them. This phenomenon isn't a coincidence; it's rooted in psychology and basic human behavior. Let's explore how adjusting your approach can shift the dynamic in your favor.

The Psychology of Interest and Value

Imagine you have two people in your life:

1. **Person A:** Someone you don't particularly care about or have any special attachment to.

2. **Person B:** Someone you're deeply interested in and want to impress.

With Person A, you act naturally. You aren't trying to impress them, so you're comfortable saying "no" or taking your time to respond to messages. Surprisingly, they start pursuing you more because you're not giving them full access to your attention, creating an air of mystery and independence. In their eyes, this self-assured behavior makes you appear more attractive.

With Person B, however, you act differently. You're eager to please, quick to respond, and willing to accommodate them at every turn. This eagerness can make you seem too available or even needy, diminishing your perceived value in their eyes. When you're overly invested, the mystery and excitement vanish, and they may start to take you for granted.

Shifting the Dynamic

To bring balance to your interactions with those you care about, consider treating them more like you would Person A—without games but with a focus on preserving your self-respect and dignity.

Here's how to apply this approach:

1. **Control Your Availability:** Don't always be available or rush to respond. Just as with Person A,

take your time. Respond when it's convenient for you, which subtly communicates that you value your time.

- **Example:** If they text you, wait a bit before replying, especially if you're busy or if it's not urgent. Responding immediately every time can signal that you're prioritizing them above your own needs and responsibilities.
- **Mathematics of Attraction:** People naturally value what they perceive as scarce. If your time is always readily available, they subconsciously devalue it. By creating a slight delay, you shift the perception from "always there" to "valued and respected," increasing their appreciation of your time.

2. **Balance Giving and Receiving:** Don't go out of your way to constantly do things for them or buy things for them. Let them invest in the relationship too.

   - **Example:** If you're always the one buying dinner or going out of your way to make plans, take a step back. Allow them to suggest a plan or take care of the next meal. This communicates that you value a balanced relationship.
   - **Mathematics of Reciprocity:** Research shows that when both parties contribute equally, they value the relationship more. If you're always giving, they won't feel the need

to reciprocate, which can lead to imbalance and underappreciation.

3. **Set Boundaries and Don't Fear Saying No:** Boundaries are essential for self-respect. If something doesn't sit right with you or makes you uncomfortable, don't be afraid to say so.

    - **Example:** Imagine they ask you for a favor you're not comfortable with, but you feel obligated to say yes. Instead, set a gentle boundary. Politely decline or suggest an alternative that works for you.

    - **Mathematics of Respect:** In relationships, mutual respect is crucial. When you establish boundaries, you communicate that your needs matter, which helps your partner respect and appreciate you more.

4. **Maintain Your Own Interests and Independence:** It's essential to have your own life outside the relationship. Keep up with your friends, hobbies, and career goals.

    - **Example:** If they want to see you every day, but you have a hobby class or plans with friends, don't cancel your plans. Keep that time for yourself. This makes you more attractive because it shows that you're a well-rounded person with a fulfilling life.

- **Mathematics of Autonomy:** Studies show that people are attracted to partners who have their own interests and lives. Independence can actually strengthen a relationship, as both partners bring unique perspectives and experiences to share.

5. **Avoid Over-Analyzing and Stay Present:** When you're deeply interested in someone, it's easy to overthink every word or action. Try to stay present and enjoy the moment rather than dissecting everything they say or do.

   - **Example:** If they don't text you back immediately, don't assume the worst. Instead, focus on your own activities and stay calm. This shows maturity and confidence, making you more appealing.

   - **Mathematics of Mystery:** When you don't over-explain or overanalyze, you maintain a certain mystery. Psychologically, people are more drawn to those who aren't an "open book" because they feel there's more to discover.

Real-Life Example: Emma and David at the Restaurant

Consider a real-life example of two couples at a restaurant. At one table, Emma and David are on a date. Emma is excited and eager to impress David. She watches him intently, smiles widely, and hangs on every word. Meanwhile, David is relaxed, not putting in as much effort, and he's more interested in his food than the conversation. Emma is over-invested, and David senses it, so he takes her attention for granted.

At the next table, Sarah and Mark sit together. Sarah is composed, focused on her food, and doesn't seem overly concerned about impressing Mark. She's enjoying herself and only occasionally engages with Mark. Mark, noticing her calm confidence, is captivated by her. He laughs at her jokes, watches her intently, and even becomes nervous, trying to impress her.

Sarah's self-respect and calm demeanor make her more attractive to Mark, who senses that she values herself and doesn't need his approval. Meanwhile, Emma's eagerness makes David feel she's too available, which reduces his motivation to pursue her.

Key Takeaways

- **Value Yourself First:** When you respect and prioritize yourself, others are more likely to respect and value you too.
- **Don't Chase; Attract:** By keeping a balanced approach, you create a natural pull in the relationship, encouraging mutual effort.

- **Maintain Mystery and Independence:** A little mystery can go a long way in sustaining interest, as it gives the other person something to discover.
- **Balance Your Investment:** Relationships thrive on mutual effort, so let them invest just as much as you do.

When you adopt a mindset of self-worth and maintain healthy boundaries, you become a person worth pursuing. This doesn't mean playing games but rather focusing on your own happiness, interests, and values. In relationships, confidence and self-respect are attractive—and they're the foundation for meaningful, balanced connections.

The Art of Caution

In relationships, it's easy to slip into the habit of giving all your energy, attention, and focus to one person. When that attention isn't reciprocated, you may find yourself scrutinizing every small action or word, seeking reassurance that you're as valued as you hope. This hyper-focus is draining, yet it can feel impossible to pull back when friends encourage you to "be patient, keep trying, put more effort in." But what if you're spending years trying to earn the approval of someone who may never fully appreciate you?

Why do so many women end up in this cycle? Often, it's because they invest every ounce of their energy into a man who may not be equally invested in them. And when he finally tires of his own pursuits, he remembers the "safe" woman waiting in the wings. **But is he coming back for love? Or simply because he no longer has anyone else?**

This is where the concept of balance and self-worth comes into play. Women who maintain lives filled with their own interests—friends, passions, and even admirers—tend to be happier and more resilient than those who give everything to one person. This doesn't mean engaging in other relationships or betraying trust. It means retaining a strong sense of self that exists independently of any man.

There's a big difference between a woman with options and a woman whose world revolves entirely around her partner. The woman with her own life remains calm, self-assured, and steady, while the woman who makes him her everything may feel anxious and unsettled, depending on his every mood. This inner stability is what draws a man in and subtly reminds him that your attention is something to be earned, not taken for granted.

The stories of two women, each on different paths:

Mona's Story

Mona was sweet and generous to a fault. When she met Saad, she fell head over heels and quickly built her life around him, setting aside her friends, family, and personal interests. Saad didn't explicitly ask her to do this, but he quickly noticed how willing she was to cater to his every preference. When he casually mentioned he liked dark hair, she dyed her blonde locks without a second thought, even though her friends told her blonde suited her best. Her life became a reflection of his tastes, not her own.

But as Mona's world shrank to the size of her relationship, Saad's respect for her began to fade. Her eagerness to please transformed her into someone he felt he could control effortlessly. The more she focused on him, the more he pulled away. Mona became consumed with trying to recapture his affection, but without other sources of fulfillment or joy, she had nothing left to draw on but him—and he grew tired of it.

Amira's Story

Amira, by contrast, maintained a sense of independence. Beautiful, confident, and ambitious, she met Thomas while traveling in Paris. They connected instantly, but Amira never allowed Thomas to become her entire world. She kept her friendships, work, and hobbies close, giving each an important place in her life. She had admirers and friends who lifted her confidence and reminded her of her value, so her self-worth wasn't tied exclusively to Thomas.

The important thing is that he gave her his number and left, and she was in control because she was the one who had his number and called him when she returned to her country two weeks later. When he first answered the call, he did not believe that she called. She was very upset and wanted to call before since he gives her his number. But She tried to control herself and be happy with her friends in Paris, and she did not even think about seeing him because she wanted to be different from the rest he meet before her, days passed, and with time she became in control as his mood depended on her calls. Amira was drowning in a sea of words of love, flirtation, tenderness, and imaginary promises, and this was crazy, and at the same time, her time was not hers because she was always busy with her boyfriend, her colleague, her friend, or something like, "**I want you to see the sea and I want you to see how I see you with my own eyes.**" He admired it and walked, He says to her, "What do you think about meeting up?" She starts giving him convincing excuses, but at the same time in a smooth and sophisticated manner. What helped her was that she didn't put all her energy into him or give him too much attention because she had alternatives that kept her busy. Amira wasn't expecting more attention from him or more sweet talk (this doesn't prevent him from wanting her, why would you expect that??? because she got it from someone else and what drives Thomas crazy is that the girl is full of attention but of confidence he doesn't know from whom so she doesn't get sensitive about trivial things and her outlook on life is terribly positive even though she also reciprocates the same feeling. Amira knew how to balance things and she also knew when to overdo it, for example if he asked to see her for the third time and she was still making excuses and felt that he was starting to get angry, here she would get ahead of him and say "What do you think about meeting up? I really miss you" and he would always forget the excuses that came before. From Amira's experience in life, she came to know who deserves it and who should close the door on him. She didn't abandon her life and Thomas was a very capable man with the second time because she simply loved herself. Thomas would always tell her "Amira, I don't know why I don't see anyone but you and I don't want anyone but you even though I got…" A million times more care, love and sacrifice from you, but I'm sure you did magic to me!! Do you know what magic is??? The precautions that Amira has!! Thomas couldn't help but be drawn to her self-assurance and independence. Whenever he started feeling she was slipping away, Amira would show him affection, but never at the expense of her own dignity or freedom. She kept parts of herself out of reach, a mystery he could never fully grasp. To Thomas, Amira was irreplaceable—a woman whose world he wanted to be a part of, but who didn't need him to feel complete.

The Lesson of Caution

Caution isn't betrayal; it's a form of self-respect. To thrive in love, a woman must remember that her worth is not defined by one relationship. She has no obligation to make any man her whole world, especially one who doesn't show her the same commitment. Keeping friends, interests, and admirers close helps her stay strong and steady, regardless of any man's attentions.

It's a subtle but essential balance. Don't allow yourself to slip into isolation, where only his approval matters. Instead, cultivate a fulfilling, multifaceted life that keeps you grounded. Hold onto your sense of self-worth and allow yourself to grow beyond any one relationship. The man who truly values you will respect that independence—and the one who doesn't isn't worth your time or energy.

Balancing With Precaution

Some believe that giving every bit of their energy to a single person is a sign of commitment, but there's a difference between devotion and over-reliance. Maintaining a balanced, fulfilling life with multiple sources of joy and connection isn't betrayal; it's a precaution that keeps you grounded and whole.

When a woman's life is full of interests, friends, and admirers, she radiates confidence and strength. Her happiness isn't tied to any one person, so if her partner disappoints her, she has plenty of ways to uplift herself. This makes her attractive and compelling in a way that total dependency never could. Conversely, when a woman puts all her emotional energy into one person, her self-worth becomes fragile, dependent on his attention and approval. This makes her vulnerable and, over time, can wear down her spirit.

Real-Life Cautionary Tales: Mesha and Amira

Mesha was a kind and giving person who met Rishi, an ambitious, attractive man. The connection was instant, and soon Mesha made him the center of her world. When Rishi casually mentioned he liked a particular thing, she'd immediately change herself or her life to match his preferences, even if it meant putting her own needs aside. When he commented on languages, she even switched her children's school to reflect his views. Soon, Rishi began to treat Mesha with indifference, feeling he could control her without any effort. Her constant compliance made him lose interest, and eventually, he found someone else. Mesha was left shattered, having given up her friends, her identity, and her energy for a man who no longer valued her.

In contrast, Amira was wise with her affections and understood the power of balance. She was ambitious, self-assured, and gave her energy to her friends, family, and hobbies—not just one man. When she met Thomas, she allowed him into her life, but didn't alter her world for him. She maintained control, keeping a sense of mystery and independence.

Thomas was captivated by Amira's unique balance of affection and self-assured distance. When he felt she might be slipping away, she would draw him back in, but never at the cost of her own identity. She became a magnetic presence he could never fully capture, and because of her independence, he respected and desired her more.

Final Thoughts

The art of caution lies in remembering that no one relationship should define your worth. Women who maintain strong connections outside of their romantic relationships remain resilient, confident, and grounded. They don't rely on one person for happiness, and this balance gives them the freedom to love without losing themselves. Love deeply, but remember to love yourself deeply, too. True happiness and stability come when you are rooted in your own strength, with love as a complement to your life—not the whole of it.

Balancing Jealousy in Relationships: Embracing Confidence and Trust

Excessive jealousy in a relationship can be damaging and, when expressed openly and frequently, often backfires, eroding confidence and trust. While a touch of jealousy can be endearing and natural, it's essential to avoid the extremes that make one seem insecure or possessive. Here's how jealousy is typically perceived and managed:

When men show jealousy, it's often seen as a protective trait, and many women accept it as part of masculine behavior. However, if a woman exhibits similar jealousy, she risks being viewed as overly controlling or insecure. It's a double standard, but it exists, and understanding this difference can help prevent misunderstandings.

Common Jealous Scenarios and Their Reactions

1. **A Beautiful Girl Passes By**
    - ***Reaction:*** "Did you notice her?" or

pointing out imagined flaws in the other woman.

- ***Better Approach:*** Act naturally. Confidently, carry on as if nothing happened, conveying that you feel secure in your relationship.

2. **An Attractive Celebrity on TV**
    - ***Reaction:*** Repeatedly asking, "Is she prettier than me?" or insisting on changing the channel.
    - ***Better Approach:*** Lighten the moment. Joke or dance playfully instead, showing that you're comfortable and not threatened.
3. **Seeing His old classmate in Public**
    - ***Reaction:*** Avoiding her out of fear he might find her attractive.
    - ***Better Approach:*** Greet her warmly, introduce her confidently, and treat her as family.
4. **His Work Involves Interactions with Women**
    - ***Reaction:*** Obsessively questioning every female colleague he interacts with.
    - ***Better Approach:*** Understand they're just colleagues, not rivals, and that his professionalism is part of who he is.
5. **If He Dresses Well to Go Out**
    - ***Reaction:*** Questioning every detail about his plans and assuming he's meeting someone else.

- ***Better Approach:*** Compliment him and encourage him to look his best. Express trust that he'll represent your relationship well.

6. **If He Travels with Friends**
   - ***Reaction:*** Calling constantly and demanding check-ins.
   - Better Approach: Show enthusiasm for his trip and encourage him to enjoy himself, fostering a sense of independence and mutual trust.
7. **Social Gatherings**
   - ***Reaction:*** Calling frequently or feeling upset when he's with friends.
   - Better Approach: Respect his time with friends and enjoy your own social life, reinforcing that you both value independence.
8. **Using His Phone Before Bed**
   - ***Reaction:*** Complaining or demanding he puts his phone away.
   - ***Better Approach:*** Let him enjoy his downtime without suspicion. Showing trust builds intimacy and mutual respect.
9. **If His Phone is Left Unattended**
   - ***Reaction:*** Going through it to find "evidence."
   - ***Better Approach:*** Respect his privacy, knowing that a secure relationship doesn't need invasive behavior.

10. **If He Compliments Another Woman Respectfully**

- ***Reaction:*** Reacting negatively or accusing him of wanting her.
- ***Better Approach:*** Acknowledge the compliment and even agree, showing that you're secure enough to recognize others' beauty.

Final Thoughts on Jealousy

Healthy relationships thrive on trust and mutual respect, not surveillance and suspicion. While jealousy can be playful when shown subtly, overdoing it makes you seem insecure and, worse, like you're impersonating a man's role rather than showing your unique strength. By responding calmly and with confidence, you'll not only preserve your dignity but also reinforce the foundation of trust in your relationship.

True stories:

Story 1: Amal and George – When Jealousy Took Over

Amal and George had a seemingly happy marriage at the start. Amal loved George deeply, but she couldn't help feeling insecure whenever he interacted with other women, even in casual or professional settings. Over time, her jealousy grew more intense; she started questioning his loyalty, checking his phone, and interrupting his conversations if a woman was present.

Despite George's reassurances, Amal's constant suspicion wore him down. Eventually, he began feeling trapped, as if nothing he did would be enough to earn her trust. The tension between them grew, and he started spending more time away, feeling unappreciated and controlled. Amal's jealousy and inability to trust eventually pushed George away, creating distance and resentment. In the end, their relationship broke down, and the marriage ended, primarily because Amal's jealousy overshadowed the love and trust that once bonded them.

Story 2: Jamila and Gamal – Staying Strong and Dignified

Jamila and Gamal had a stable marriage, but Gamal, tempted by the attention he received from a well-known TV anchor, made a mistake and had an affair. Jamila had her suspicions but chose not to confront Gamal directly. Instead, she focused on keeping her home in order, nurturing her children, and taking care of herself. She maintained her dignity, appearing calm and unbothered, and continued living her life confidently and happily.

Gamal, on the other hand, felt guilty and fearful that Jamila might find out. In an attempt to compensate, he showered her with gifts, planned family holidays, and ensured she felt appreciated. This strategy allowed Jamila to live comfortably and confidently, enjoying the fruits of her husband's guilt-driven generosity while he, in turn, grew to appreciate her grace and resilience. Over time, Gamal began to see Jamila's strength and the unwavering dignity she brought to their household. He realized her inner beauty and loyalty far outweighed any fleeting thrill from the affair, and he grew to regret his actions, ultimately valuing and respecting her even more.

Here are three different examples that illustrate how balanced responses to jealousy can strengthen a relationship:

Example 1: When He Looks at Another Woman

- ***Unbalanced Reaction:*** Asking repeatedly, "**Did you notice her?**" or criticizing the other woman to draw his attention back.
- ***Balanced Reaction:*** Smile confidently and carry on with the conversation. This shows you're secure in the relationship, making it clear that you trust his commitment to you.

Example 2: When He's Going Out with Friends

- ***Unbalanced Reaction:*** Calling him every hour, asking who he's with, or feeling upset that he didn't invite you.
- ***Balanced Reaction:*** Encourage him to enjoy his time, and maybe make plans with your own

friends. This reinforces mutual trust and respect for each other's independence.

Example 3: When He Praises Another Woman's Appearance

- ***Unbalanced Reaction:*** Responding with suspicion or saying, "If you like her so much, go be with her!"
- ***Balanced Reaction:*** Agree with him or acknowledge the compliment with a light-hearted remark. Showing you're not threatened by his admiration of someone else's beauty reinforces your confidence and security.

Chapter 4

Challenging Situations

Facing Fear: When and Why a Man May Fear Certain Women

Many women wonder why men sometimes pull away in relationships, even when they seem to be enchanted by the woman they're with. A lot of women will recognize this: they find themselves suddenly wondering, *What did I do wrong? Is he losing interest?* But often, it's not that simple. Some men start to retreat when they meet a woman who is particularly extraordinary, someone who seems to "have it all." This reaction is rooted in fear—fear of falling too hard, fear of being vulnerable, or fear of losing control. In this chapter, we'll explore how and why this dynamic unfolds, using real examples and clear explanations.

Why Do Men Sometimes Fear Falling for an Extraordinary Woman?

Imagine a man, Sam, who enters a relationship with a woman, Sarah, who seems perfect in his eyes. She's smart, attractive, charismatic, and full of life. Sarah stands out from others—she has an effortless charm and a sense of self-worth that makes her magnetic. Sam is initially thrilled and

can't believe his luck. He's proud to be with her, constantly calling and showing her off to his friends. But over time, something changes. He begins to pull back, becoming distant and harder to reach.
Sarah notices this shift and starts to wonder if she's done something wrong.

But here's the surprising truth: Sam hasn't lost interest. In fact, he's likely fallen for Sarah more deeply than he planned, and he's afraid of those feelings. Here are some thoughts he might have:

- *"She's incredibly independent and doesn't rely on me; she could leave anytime. Am I vulnerable here?"*
- *"What if I lose myself in this relationship? I've always been the one in control."*
- *"I can't stop thinking about her, and it scares me. I don't want to be that guy who's overly attached."*

This reaction is common with men who are used to staying emotionally guarded. When they meet a woman who truly captivates them, they sometimes retreat to avoid feeling "trapped" by their emotions. In some cases, they withdraw because they can't believe they're good enough for her, or they fear she'll eventually realize she could do better.

How Do Men Act When They Feel Intimidated by a Woman?

Here are some real statements from men describing how they feel and act when they're falling for a woman who seems "too perfect" for them:

1. **Pulling Back on Purpose**

   "If I feel I've given too much to a girl who's exactly my type, I'll start calling less. I want her to miss me, to see what it's like when I'm not there." — *Steve*

2. **Acting Disinterested**

   "I can't let her know she's on my mind all the time, so I pretend I'm busy with other things. But I'm actually struggling to keep my thoughts off her." — *Jake*

3. **Playing It Cool**

   "Sometimes I try to show her that I'm fine without her, that she doesn't have me wrapped around her finger. I act as if I'm not bothered, but the truth is, I can't get her out of my head." — *Mike*

4. **Becoming Cold**

   "When I'm really into a girl, I'll start acting colder, even distant. It's my way of fighting my own emotions." — *Paul*

5. **Avoiding Her Altogether**

"There are times I don't even want to see her because I know I'm already infatuated. I make excuses not to meet because I'm worried it'll only get stronger." — *Frank*

What Should a Woman Do in These Situations?

When a man pulls back like this, it's easy for a woman to feel insecure, to start questioning herself or overthinking what went wrong. But in reality, this reaction from him is often a compliment—it means he finds you remarkable, even overwhelming in the best way. Here's how to navigate this phase without losing your confidence or getting caught up in his emotional push-and-pull:

1. **Don't Change Yourself**

Remember that he fell for you as you are. His sudden distance isn't a reflection of something you did wrong; it's often his way of dealing with unexpected feelings. Stay true to yourself, and don't try to dim your light just because he's afraid to see it shine.

2. **Give Him Space Without Pulling Away**

You don't need to chase him or demand his attention. Stay present, but avoid pushing for answers or trying to "fix" his uncertainty. Your calm presence will reassure him that you're confident in yourself and in the relationship.

3. **Stay Unpredictable and Engaging**

Men often fear monotony or feeling too comfortable too quickly. Keep being the woman who is full of life, intelligence, and charm. Challenge him, keep him guessing, and let him realize that he has to put in effort to win you fully.

Examples: How Women Navigate This Dynamic

Example 1: Laura and Tom

Laura is a confident, independent woman who has a contagious smile and a sharp wit. Tom is drawn to her but starts to feel overwhelmed by how effortlessly she seems to shine. He's used to being in control, and with Laura, he feels vulnerable. He pulls back, becoming less communicative. Laura notices but decides not to confront him. Instead, she keeps living her life, going out with friends, pursuing her interests, and staying friendly with him without being overly available. Over time, Tom's fear subsides as he realizes she's secure in herself—and that she doesn't need him but wants him. Her calm and confident attitude keeps him intrigued and eventually brings him closer.

Example 2: Emily and Adam

Emily is in a relationship with Adam, who is known for his wandering eye. At first, it bothers her when he glances at other women, but she decides to handle it differently. One day, when they're out together, Emily casually glances at an attractive man nearby. Adam notices but says nothing. The next time he glances at another woman, Emily doesn't react. Over time, Adam becomes more focused on her, realizing she isn't going to compete for his attention—and that she's strong and self-assured. Emily's calm confidence teaches Adam to respect her, and he becomes more attentive.

Example 3: Kate and Ben

Kate is dating Ben, who has a tendency to complain about how "all girls are after him." Instead of reacting with jealousy or insecurity, Kate laughs it off, saying, "Well, lucky for me, I'm different." She doesn't feed into his need to feel desired by everyone else, and her unbothered attitude makes him appreciate her unique personality. He gradually drops the act, realizing he doesn't need to prove his worth to her; she values him just as he is.

Key Takeaways: How to Keep His Interest Without Chasing

- **Maintain Your Mystery**

Men often crave the thrill of the chase. Let him work to understand you. Be open, but don't reveal every thought or feeling. Create an element of surprise that keeps him coming back for more.

- **Stay Confident in Yourself**

His actions are often more about his own insecurities than anything you've done. When you stay steady and sure of yourself, he'll eventually recognize and value your strength.

- **Don't Seek Validation from Him**

Men respect women who are comfortable in their own skin and don't need constant reassurance. Enjoy your own life, build your own happiness, and he'll be drawn to your self-assuredness.

By recognizing these patterns, you can feel empowered in your relationship, knowing his fear or distance is often a sign of his deep interest. Your calm, confident approach will either bring him closer or, at the very least, allow you to feel at peace with yourself, knowing you stayed true to who you are.

Additional Examples: How Women Navigate the Dynamics of Male Fear and Withdrawal

Example 1: Laura and Tom

Laura is a confident, independent woman with a thriving career and active social life. Tom, initially captivated by her strength and charm, finds himself feeling more vulnerable than he's used to. He begins pulling back, almost testing Laura to see if she'll notice or become overly concerned about his distance.

Laura, however, handles it with quiet composure. She doesn't chase after him or ask why he's pulling away. Instead, she remains present in the relationship but continues living her life as she did before, spending time with friends, pursuing her interests, and staying positive. Her self-assured attitude conveys that while she values Tom, she doesn't need constant reassurance from him.

Over time, Tom's fears begin to dissolve as he realizes that her independence doesn't mean she's detached or uninterested. Her calm confidence shows him that he has to actively choose to be part of her life—a realization that draws him closer, ultimately deepening their bond.

Example 2: Emily and Adam

Emily and Adam have been dating for a few months when she notices Adam's habit of checking out other women. At first, she feels insecure, wondering if she isn't enough. But rather than letting this get to her, Emily takes a different approach. One day, while they're out, she notices Adam's wandering eye and simply glances at an attractive man nearby without a word.

Adam catches this and, while he doesn't say anything, he becomes more attentive. He realizes Emily isn't competing for his validation—she's secure enough to know her own worth and doesn't let his behavior unsettle her. Gradually, Adam's attention centers more fully on Emily, respecting the confidence she exudes by staying true to herself.

Key Takeaways for Women in Navigating Male Fears:

- **Maintain a Sense of Mystery**

  Men often crave the thrill of discovering who you are over time. Let him get to know you at a natural pace, revealing layers gradually rather than all at once. This mystery sustains his curiosity and interest.

- **Don't Depend on His Validation**

  Building your own happiness and pursuing personal goals creates a powerful attraction. Men respect women who are confident on their own terms, without constantly seeking validation from a relationship.

- **Demonstrate Calm Confidence**

  By staying grounded and true to yourself during his moments of withdrawal, you show him you're not afraid of his doubts or insecurities. This unshakeable presence is both compelling and reassuring, often inspiring him to overcome his fears and draw closer.

These examples and insights add depth to the theme of how women can navigate a man's fears while maintaining their self-worth and independence. This approach strengthens the relationship by making it clear that confidence and self-assurance are key to sustaining an unbreakable bond.

The Complex World of Betrayal

When we spoke before, we discussed lighthearted mischief—harmless instances where a man might act impulsively. But betrayal, especially deep and ongoing betrayal, runs much deeper than this. Many people, particularly in the Gulf region, experience such major betrayals, and understanding the causes of these behaviors reveals layers far more profound than casual flirtation or glances. To understand betrayal fully, we need to examine its roots and define it in ways that go beyond surface-level interpretations.

Betrayal, when mentioned, often evokes a singular image of deceit. Yet, it's not as simple as a stray glance or brief encounter. There are different forms of betrayal, each carrying its own weight and impact. Before we delve into these types, let's address the underlying causes. Why does betrayal occur in the first place?

Causes of Betrayal

Often, a man will seek a "safe" relationship with a woman he perceives as loyal, unchallenging, and steadfast—someone he feels certain won't cause him heartbreak or demand too much emotional investment. He may stay with her while indulging in a separate life, free of the restraints he associates with that "safe" partner. This other life offers him a space to be carefree, adventurous, and uninhibited, which he may not feel he can experience in the same way with his primary partner.

This is where the disconnect begins. The woman in the stable relationship believes she has found a partner for life and is content within the boundaries she has set for herself and for the relationship. Meanwhile, the man is harboring a separate world of thrill and indulgence that he shares with someone else, a partner who mirrors his pursuit of freedom and excitement. This duplicity leaves the loyal partner as a mere placeholder, someone not truly integrated into the man's full world.

Over time, as the woman begins to express her emotions and her desire for deeper connection, the dynamic shifts. What began as a seemingly balanced relationship starts to unravel. Her expressions of love and her attempts to seek validation become, to him, a source of frustration. He perceives her needs as "drama," and the relationship turns cold and unfulfilling.

The Two Faces of Betrayal: Physical and Emotional

Let's break down betrayal into two significant categories:

1. Physical Betrayal

Physical betrayal often gets the most attention and causes immense distress. If a woman discovers that her partner has been unfaithful in this way, her initial response might be to confront him directly. However, handling this situation with patience can often yield better results. Rather than reacting immediately, which can lead the partner to downplay the situation or manipulate the truth, a calm, steady response gives the woman an upper hand. She can let her partner feel the weight of his actions by subtly shifting her demeanor, making him question what she knows or suspects without outright confrontation. This way, he's kept on edge, worried about potential consequences, and becomes more cautious.

However, if she does confront him openly and gives him an ultimatum, she risks creating a cycle where he simply becomes better at hiding his actions, knowing the worst she'll do is forgive him again. Thus, for minor incidents, silence and calculated detachment can have a stronger impact, making him aware that his actions do not go unnoticed but sparing her the potential agony of repeated disappointments.

2. Emotional Betrayal

Emotional betrayal is far more devastating. When a man finds himself emotionally involved with another woman, it's no longer about physical impulses—it's about his heart. If this happens, the woman has only one viable option: to leave. No amount of pleading or compromise will ever fully bring him back, because his emotions have shifted. Continuing to cling to him only prolongs her suffering and diminishes her dignity.

This kind of betrayal runs deep, and even if the man calls or attempts to mend things, it's usually just to soothe his own conscience, not out of genuine love or regret. As many writers poignantly expressed, sometimes distance is a more beautiful form of love.

How to Recognize Reckless Betrayal: A Real Story

One example of physical betrayal underlines just how deceptive and manipulative a partner can become. In this real story, Lora was in a relationship with Benjamin, a man she deeply loved and trusted. They had built a life together, living in Paris while pursuing their studies. Lora believed she had found a partner who matched her dreams—a man who respected her and shared her ambitions.

But soon, cracks began to show. Benjamin often went out at night, claiming he was studying with friends, yet his behavior didn't align with someone engrossed in academics. He dressed sharply, wore expensive cologne, and stayed out until dawn. Suspicious but unwilling to strain their relationship further, Lora kept her concerns to herself. However, her instincts were right—something was amiss.

One night, she decided to follow him, disguising herself and observing his whereabouts. What she discovered was beyond anything she could have imagined: Benjamin was indeed with his "friends," but they were gathered in a nightclub, surrounded by other women. The scene was unmistakable. lora, however, kept her composure. She returned home, saying nothing, and formulated a plan.

Over the following weeks, she sent Benjamin anonymous letters demanding money in exchange for "secrecy," threatening to expose him if he didn't comply. The psychological strain wore him down, and soon he found himself too anxious and financially drained to continue his nightly escapades. In the end, Benjamin's betrayal cost him dearly, and it was only due to Lora's patience and strategic thinking that she was able to protect herself from further hurt.

A Final Word on Self-Worth

In cases of betrayal, it's essential to maintain a sense of self-worth and dignity. Whether the betrayal is physical or emotional, women should remember that they have the power to choose their response. Rather than becoming consumed by the betrayal or attempting to salvage a broken relationship at any cost, sometimes the best option is to let go and seek a fresh start. Betrayal is painful, but it can also be a catalyst for growth, strength, and the realization that self-respect should never be compromised for the sake of someone unwilling to reciprocate loyalty and love.

Ultimately, in situations of betrayal, remaining calm, centered, and aware of one's own value offers a path to healing and, eventually, to a life free of those who do not appreciate or deserve the love and trust given to them.

The Weight of Betrayal: Lessons from Real Stories

When dealing with betrayal, it's essential to use both wisdom and self-respect. Reacting without thought or letting emotions take control often leads to deeper hurt and entrapment. Through the stories of two women, Mercedes and Sophia, we see two very different approaches to betrayal, with two very different outcomes. Their stories reveal valuable lessons on handling betrayal wisely and preserving one's dignity.

Mercedes' Story: Winning Through Self-Control

Mercedes' experience shows the power of patience and self-control. She discovered that her partner, Alex, was being unfaithful. But instead of reacting immediately, she kept her composure and developed a strategy to stay in control. She observed him discreetly, gathering evidence but choosing not to confront him outright. Mercedes avoided a direct confrontation, instead subtly letting Alex know she was aware of his behavior without giving him the satisfaction of seeing her hurt. This kept him on edge, uncertain about her next move, and ultimately forced him to adjust his actions.

Lesson: Mercedes' approach shows that sometimes it's wiser not to confront betrayal directly. By handling the situation calmly and without drama, she protected her dignity and left Alex in a position of worry and regret.

Sophia's Story: The Cost of Letting Emotions Rule

Sophia's approach was quite different. She allowed her emotions to dictate her actions, repeatedly forgiving her partner, James, even after he consistently disrespected her. James was evasive and unfaithful, but Sophia kept going back to him, hoping he would finally commit. Her deep affection for him overruled her sense of self-respect, and she spent sleepless nights waiting for him, calling him obsessively, and even waiting outside his home when she suspected he was with someone else. Each time, James dismissed her, knowing he held control over her.

Lesson: Sophia's story highlights the danger of letting emotions lead when facing betrayal. By showing James how deeply she cared, she gave him the power to manipulate her repeatedly, leaving her hurt and humiliated while he continued his behavior without remorse.

Key Lessons on Handling Betrayal

1. **Stay Calm and Strategic:** Reacting impulsively often makes betrayal worse. Instead, take a step back, assess the situation, and consider how best to protect yourself. This could mean observing quietly, as Mercedes did, or deciding to leave if the betrayal is severe.

2. **Value Yourself First:** Don't let your self-worth depend on someone else's behavior. If a partner is unfaithful, prioritize your own dignity. Sophia's

repeated forgiveness only encouraged James to continue mistreating her.

3. **Set Boundaries and Stick to Them:** Clearly define what is acceptable and what isn't. If a partner crosses that line, know when to walk away. Mercedes handled betrayal on her terms, keeping Alex in check without letting him take advantage of her.

4. **Avoid Letting Emotions Cloud Your Judgment:** Emotional reactions often lead to regrets. If you find yourself overly affected by a partner's betrayal, take time to detach and approach the situation with a clear head. In Sophia's case, emotional over-investment only led to more heartbreak.

Other Examples of Betrayal and How to Respond

Yasmine's Story: Subtle Manipulation and False Hope

Yasmine's story is a cautionary tale of misplaced loyalty. She fell deeply in love with Liam, a man who didn't value her. She gave up her goals and dreams to be with him, only to discover that he had no intention of reciprocating her loyalty. Liam was in love with another woman, Claire, who he considered his true soulmate. Though married to Yasmine, Liam continued to prioritize Claire emotionally, leaving Yasmine feeling like an afterthought.

Lesson: If someone truly loves you, they won't make you feel like an option. Yasmine sacrificed her dreams, hoping for love in return, but ended up disappointed. Relationships should be built on mutual respect and shared commitment—not sacrifice and one-sided devotion.

Claire's Story: Seeing Through Superficial Apologies

Claire was married to a man who repeatedly lied about his actions, promising to change each time she caught him being dishonest. He would apologize profusely and swear he wouldn't repeat his behavior, only to go back on his word once he felt secure in the relationship again. Claire's forgiving nature kept her trapped in a cycle of deceit and heartbreak.

Lesson: Be wary of repeated apologies without action. If someone is truly remorseful, they will work consistently to change their behavior. If they don't, then the relationship may not be worth the pain of staying. Trust actions over words.

Thoughts and Advice

In relationships, betrayal is painful and often inevitable at some point, but how we respond defines our self-worth and future happiness. It's essential to remember that:

- **Self-respect comes first:** No one deserves to be treated as an option, and we each have the power to choose how we respond to betrayal.

- **Set boundaries and keep them:** Avoid bending your values or sacrificing your dreams for someone who wouldn't do the same for you.
- **Choose carefully whom you give second chances:** If a partner is genuinely sorry, they will show change without needing constant forgiveness.

Taking these lessons to heart can help you not only handle betrayal but also emerge stronger, wiser, and more confident. Every challenge can be a chance to grow and strengthen your own sense of self-worth. Remember, life is too short to wait on someone who doesn't truly value your love and loyalty. Choose dignity over doubt, respect over resentment, and the freedom to be with someone who truly deserves you.

The Complexity of Pleasing a Man: Understanding the "Mop Woman" and the "Idolized Man"

Many relationships fall into the same predictable cycle, where one partner (often the woman) gives everything to keep the other satisfied, only to find that her sacrifices go unnoticed or even unappreciated. This scenario often involves a "mop woman"—someone who gives, sacrifices, and supports endlessly—while the man becomes her idol, a figure whose approval she constantly chases but rarely secures. Let's explore the layers of this dynamic, the psychological toll it takes, and the reasons why, despite her sacrifices, the "idolized" man rarely feels fulfilled or satisfied.

1. The Sacrifice Cycle: Why the "Mop Woman" Feels Unseen

In this dynamic, the woman feels compelled to put her partner's needs and desires above her own, often to extremes. She will sacrifice her time, aspirations, and sometimes her identity, all in the hope of winning his admiration or gratitude. She believes that if she does enough—if she works tirelessly to smooth over conflicts, to make his life comfortable, to always agree with him—he will finally see her as irreplaceable. But her efforts don't seem to matter, and he grows accustomed to her sacrifices, feeling entitled rather than appreciative.

The reason? The human psyche doesn't naturally reward someone for what they have given consistently and without question. Instead, value often grows through challenge and limitation.

A man who perceives his partner as always available and sacrificially loyal may feel a strange mix of indifference and entitlement. He comes to expect her dedication as a baseline, not an effort. For him, there's no mystery, no thrill in a person who gives without hesitation, and the dynamic leaves her feeling drained and invisible, despite all her efforts.

2. The Idolization Trap: When Everything Revolves Around Him

When a woman idolizes her partner, she places him at the center of her world, shaping her actions and emotions around his mood and reactions.

If he's pleased, she feels a brief high, as though she's succeeded. But the satisfaction is fleeting because his expectations continue to grow, and any minor "mistake" on her part feels like a massive failure.

The smallest mistake can feel like a catastrophe, leading her to seek redemption through yet another series of sacrifices. This is emotionally exhausting, and over time, she loses her sense of self-worth. Her happiness is no longer based on her own accomplishments or personal fulfillment but entirely on his approval.

Meanwhile, he often sees her devotion not as a form of love but as a sign of dependency. He may feel a sense of power, even superiority, in the relationship, knowing she will always yield to his needs. Ironically, this very dependency—this devotion without boundaries—can become unappealing.

The relationship starts to lack a sense of adventure or equal partnership, and he may begin to withdraw, taking her devotion for granted while seeking excitement or challenge elsewhere.

3. Independence vs. Dependency: The Thrill of an Independent Partner

Men often feel drawn to partners who maintain a sense of independence and mystery. An independent partner doesn't orbit around his every move or mood. She has her own dreams, her own life, and doesn't depend on him for validation. This autonomy creates a kind of balance, a push and pull, that keeps the relationship dynamic and engaging. She is not afraid to voice her opinions or assert her boundaries, and this quality can be incredibly attractive because it shows confidence and self-worth.

In contrast, a partner who seeks constant approval may become predictable, leaving the man feeling stagnant. He may even feel a sense of "ownership" over her, reducing the relationship to a one-sided dependency. The paradox is that, though he may not consciously realize it, he craves a relationship where his partner's love is neither guaranteed nor unconditional—where there's a sense of excitement, possibility, and even risk.

4. Keeping Mystery and Confidence: Why Adventure Matters

In healthy relationships, there's an element of unpredictability. This doesn't mean instability but rather a level of challenge that keeps both partners invested. When a woman maintains her own identity and passions, she invites her partner into her world rather than revolving around his.

She challenges him, disagrees with him, and expresses her true self. This unpredictability fuels a sense of adventure, keeping the relationship fresh.

For instance, consider a woman who has her own career, interests, and social life. She doesn't ask her partner's opinion on every small decision; instead, she acts with confidence, knowing her worth. She may share her world with him but does not become consumed by his. This independence creates a relationship dynamic that is both respectful and inspiring. Her partner may even feel a healthy sense of "chase," as he realizes that her love is a choice, not a given. Her individuality keeps him intrigued and committed, as he recognizes her as an equal, not someone dependent on his approval.

5. True Partnership: Embracing Equality and Mutual Respect

The healthiest relationships are those where both partners view each other as equals, and their connection is built on mutual admiration rather than a need for validation. In a true partnership, there's no "mop woman" sacrificing for a man who sits on a pedestal. Instead, both partners bring their full selves to the relationship, supporting one another while maintaining their own independence.

Here, love is not a transaction but an exchange of respect, empathy, and genuine admiration. When a woman embraces her own value, she sets boundaries, says no when needed, and does not bend her life to fit someone else's. Her partner, in turn, learns to value her strength and independence, understanding that he must be worthy of her affection. This balance keeps the relationship grounded, respectful, and ultimately fulfilling for both.

6. The Danger of Society's Expectations

Society often pressures women to adopt the "mop" role in relationships, encouraging self-sacrifice, humility, and a need to please others. These expectations can create a mindset where a woman feels she must prove her worth through service to her partner, giving until she's empty. However, no one benefits from this dynamic, least of all the woman herself. She loses sight of her individuality, and the relationship becomes unsatisfying for both partners.

True fulfillment comes when a woman follows her own path, refusing to bend to social expectations or define her worth through a partner. By cultivating her own life and self-respect, she establishes a foundation that invites equal respect from others. In this way, she is not only a stronger individual but a more fulfilling partner, bringing authenticity rather than compliance to her relationships.

The Takeaway: Be Your Own Center

The essence of a balanced and satisfying relationship lies in self-worth and mutual respect. When a woman becomes her own center—valuing her independence, prioritizing her happiness, and pursuing her goals—she offers her partner something far more valuable than constant devotion. She brings him a dynamic partnership, where both partners are free to grow, support each other, and maintain a sense of adventure.

Remember: love isn't about idolizing another person or being idolized. It's about recognizing that a healthy relationship doesn't require you to sacrifice your self-respect or abandon your individuality. A true partnership allows you to be complete in yourself while enjoying the presence of someone who respects you for who you truly are.

How to Navigate the Difficult Phase After a Breakup

The period after a breakup can be incredibly challenging, and it's completely natural to feel lost, overwhelmed, or even paralyzed. During this time, you may feel as if the world is closing in around you, making it hard to breathe or think clearly and some women choose to shorten their hair or change it's colour. Despite the support of friends and loved ones, it can be difficult to shake the sadness. It's essential to understand that these feelings are normal. Many people have experienced the same pain, emerged stronger, and found happiness with someone new. In fact, most people eventually look back and wonder why they once felt so deeply affected. Here are four steps to help you move forward and find peace during this difficult stage.

1. Allow Yourself to Feel Without Trying to Erase Memories

You may have heard advice to delete all photos, messages, and even block your ex's social media accounts to forget them. While this may work for some, it's not a one-size-fits-all solution. Deleting everything connected to them may only intensify your thoughts and reinforce a sense of loss. Instead, allow yourself to keep these things as they are. Avoid obsessively following their updates, but don't pressure yourself to erase every trace of them, either. Blocking them or engaging in dramatic actions only highlights their significance in your life. So, leave things as they are and focus on gently moving forward without a drastic purge.

2. Release Your Emotions Fully and Honestly

Suppressing your emotions, whether sadness, anger, or frustration, can backfire and increase your pain in the long run. Don't deny or downplay your feelings by saying things like, "I'm fine," or, "It's better this way." Acknowledge the emotions as they come. This person, even if they didn't end up being the right one, played a role in your life, so it's only natural to feel strongly. Cry if you need to, allow yourself to feel what's real, and embrace the sadness as a means of healing. Honest expression, rather than repression, will ultimately help you let go.

3. Confide in Your Friends and Loved Ones

Talking about your feelings with friends and family is an effective way to process and release what's inside. Don't shy away from sharing your true emotions—even the difficult or vulnerable ones. Being honest with yourself and others allows you to fully understand your feelings and avoid carrying unspoken burdens. Imagine it's like cleaning out a closet to make space for new, brighter things. Even if your friends start to grow weary of hearing about it, kindly ask for their patience. Releasing these thoughts will free up your heart and mind for new experiences, just as emptying out old clothes creates room in a closet.

4. Focus on Self-Care and Self-Improvement

Take extra care of yourself during this period, both physically and mentally. It's easy to fall into unhealthy habits—overeating, isolating yourself, or neglecting your appearance—but these will only add to your struggle. Instead, challenge yourself to focus on self-improvement as a path to happiness and renewal. Spend time outdoors, enjoy the fresh air, and take up activities that make you feel good about yourself, like trying a new hairstyle, eating healthier, or simply treating yourself to small luxuries. These actions affirm your resilience and help you rebuild your confidence, reminding you that no setback can truly break you.

A Key Consideration: Responding If Your Ex Reaches Out

Once you're on the path to healing, you might be surprised by an unexpected message or call from your ex, as this happens in many cases. If this occurs, think carefully about your response. Here are some guiding principles to keep in mind:

- **Consider the Reason for the Breakup:** If the breakup stemmed from personal harm or a breach of trust, be cautious about re-engaging. If the reason was less personal or intense, allow yourself to evaluate their intentions.
- **Take Your Time and Set Boundaries:** Don't feel compelled to jump back into the relationship. Approach it gradually, showing that you're thoughtful and intentional. Give yourself the freedom to set boundaries.
- **Don't Show Excessive Enthusiasm:** While it's okay to feel excited about reconnecting, try not to be overly eager. Remember that you've grown since the breakup, and any reconnection should acknowledge that growth.

Ultimately, any contact with an ex should be on your terms. If they wish to re-enter your life, let them meet the stronger, wiser version of you that emerged from this experience. Embrace the opportunity to make choices that align with your self-worth and well-being.

Navigating the Difficult Phase After a Breakup for Families with Children

The period following a breakup can be particularly challenging for parents and children. Separation affects not only you but also your children, who may feel deeply unsettled by the change in the family. It's completely normal to feel lost or overwhelmed. Feelings of sadness or even disorientation affect not only the parents but also the children, as they are often thrust into an environment of uncertainty. Here are steps to navigate this period while supporting your children and caring for yourself.

1. Allow Your Children to Express Their Emotions

As with yourself, it's essential to let your children freely express their feelings. Rather than telling them "everything will be fine" or trying to downplay the situation, encourage them to express what they're feeling. They may feel anger, sadness, or even guilt about the separation. Validate their emotions without judgment and explain that having strong feelings is natural in moments like these. By showing that you are also affected but resolved to move forward, you model healthy emotional management.

2. Maintain Open Communication with Your Children

Talk about the situation honestly, in a way that's appropriate for the child's age. Explain what will change and what will remain the same. Clear conversations adapted to their level of understanding can help children feel more secure. Answer their questions, even the difficult ones, to ease their worries. A child who understands better what's happening is less likely to feel confused or anxious about the changes ahead.

3. Create Stability and Routine

A child's world is often built around routine. During this time of upheaval, do your best to maintain a stable structure in their daily lives. Continue activities they enjoy, whether it's regular family meals, outings to the park, or family playtime. A stable routine helps children regain a sense of security and predictability, which can soothe their anxiety about the family changes.

4. Take Care of Yourself for Your Children's Well-Being

Taking care of yourself may seem selfish, but it's essential so you can be fully present for your children. Take time to manage your own emotions by talking to friends, seeing a therapist, or doing activities that bring you peace. Children notice and feel their parents' stress, and by caring for yourself, you show them that it's possible to overcome hard times and recover. Your well-being directly affects their own ability to handle the situation.

An Important Consideration: Communication with the Ex-Partner

When it comes to interactions with your ex-partner, it's crucial to maintain a peaceful environment for the children's sake. If messages or calls from your ex come through, first check in with your own emotions and respond in a way that won't place the children in a loyalty conflict. Here are some principles for handling this communication:

- **Remember the reasons for the separation:** If the breakup involved major issues, be cautious about the intensity of interactions.
- **Set clear boundaries:** Don't feel obligated to be available all the time. Establish guidelines to avoid ambiguity.
- Avoid showing too much enthusiasm if contact is reestablished. Show that you are moving forward for your own well-being and your children's.

Ultimately, whether or not your ex returns to your life, focus on creating a harmonious home for yourself and your children. Separation is an opportunity to show your children resilience, personal growth, and the importance of self-care and caring for others.

Why Did He Leave Me and Disappear? Was It My Fault?

It's a question many women find themselves asking at some point: "Why did he leave without an explanation?" You might wonder if you made a mistake or if there's something wrong with you, someone told him something. This confusion is natural and common. Sometimes, the fault is on our side, while other times, it's due to issues on his part. Understanding this can help you reflect on what happened without blaming yourself or holding on to someone who may not deserve your energy.

Respect yourself, knowing he may not be worthy of your feelings. Asking yourself, "What did I do wrong?" can sometimes lead you into self-blame, forgetting that he may be the one who lost out, while you've gained valuable self-awareness. Countless women share this question, which is why we want to delve deeper. Let's explore the reasons why men sometimes vanish without a word, helping you understand what happened without blaming yourself unnecessarily.

Example: Amélie and Louis

Amélie met Louis, and in the beginning, they were elated, like a perfect match. Amélie was thrilled to be with someone who seemed to truly care for her. She even began to dream of a future with him, as so many of us do. But as time passed, Louis began to pull away without any explanation. Amélie found herself wondering, "What did I do to make him leave?"

After examining her relationship and learning from the experience, she recognized the lessons she needed to carry forward, treating her time with Louis as preparation for a more fulfilling, lasting relationship that eventually arrived.

Many women face situations like Amélie's, often worse, where the man disappears suddenly. How a man leaves often depends on his personality—if he dislikes confrontation, he might disappear without a word. Or, he may gradually withdraw, giving subtle signals rather than addressing the issue directly. Whatever the case, knowing the reason behind his behavior is less important than focusing on any mistakes that could help you grow.

Common Reasons Why He May Have Left

Reason 1: You Became an Open Book Too Quickly

A mistake many women make is revealing too much too soon. Letting him know everything about you right away can remove the sense of intrigue and discovery. Men, by nature, often enjoy the excitement of uncovering layers. So, don't feel obligated to give him all the details right away. Allowing him to pursue you keeps the spark alive.

Reason 2: You Didn't Bring Challenge or Adventure to the Relationship

The excitement of challenge is a powerful motivator for many men. Challenge doesn't mean confrontation or head-to-head competition; it means maintaining a bit of mystery and confidence in yourself. Relationships aren't about arriving at a final destination; they're an ongoing dance of interest and intrigue. When he senses that the excitement has plateaued, he may lose interest.

Reason 3: You Gave Him Everything Too Easily

Many men are willing to go to great lengths for something meaningful, but if they feel they've "won" too soon, they may lose the drive to stay invested. Don't assume his initial efforts mean he'll stay as engaged without the thrill of continued discovery. If he loses interest after achieving his goals, he may drift away, realizing there's no more depth to explore. This is a sign he may have been more interested in the chase than in a genuine connection.

Reason 4: You Took a Dominant or Controlling Role Too Early

Early in a relationship, it's tempting to make suggestions or impose ideas, but often this can make him feel pressured or criticized. Men, like anyone, appreciate a sense of autonomy, even if they seem open to suggestions. Showing him respect and freedom while maintaining control quietly can create a healthy balance.

Example: Camille and Julien. Camille loved Julien deeply, and at first, he was infatuated with her. However, as she began to direct his daily choices, he felt his independence slipping. Over time, he pulled away, seeking someone who let him feel a sense of control. Camille realized later that her intense need for certainty may have been off-putting and learned to maintain balance in her next relationship.

Reason 5: Misinterpreting "Holding On as Long as You Can"

Many women believe that "holding on" means lowering their standards or sacrificing their dignity to win a man's affection. However, staying strong doesn't mean compromising your values; it means staying true to yourself. By doing this, he'll either recognize your strength or move on, leaving you with your self-respect intact.

The Greatest Mistake: Losing Yourself in Him

A relationship should enhance your life, not become your entire life. If you give up your passions, hobbies, or friendships, it places a heavy burden on him to be your sole source of joy. Many men admire a woman with a fulfilling life outside the relationship; it keeps things fresh and balanced.

Instead, keep your world full, with him as an addition rather than the sole focus. This shows him that he's with someone confident, happy, and whole—qualities that encourage a strong, lasting connection.

A breakup or sudden disappearance may be painful, but it offers valuable insights. Understanding common mistakes can help you avoid them in the future, turning these experiences into stepping stones for growth and better connections. Let go of self-blame, respect your own worth, and recognize that each experience brings you closer to finding the partner who truly deserves you.

Rising from a breakup can be a powerful journey of self-discovery and empowerment, especially for women facing financial challenges. Instead of letting the pain hold you back, use it as fuel to dive into valuable pursuits that strengthen your independence. Studying, building skills, and setting goals allow you to focus on growth and reshape your self-image. Invest time in understanding yourself and honing your abilities so that you emerge stronger and wiser.

For women with children, this is about more than personal healing; it's about standing firm for their future and yours. By committing to learning how to manage finances, work independently, and generate income, you free yourself from any control that a partner may have tried to exert.

This path may be challenging, but with determination, you can build a secure, self-sufficient life, showing both yourself and your children that strength, resilience, and independence are the foundation of true success.

Duchess Nivin ElGamal: A Testament of Strength, Advocacy, and Self-Determination

In 2003, Duchess Nivin ElGamal met Ahmed, and by 2007, she believed she had found her soulmate. With dreams of a perfect life, they married and welcomed a child into the world. But beneath the surface, her trust and kindness were met with betrayal. While she dedicated herself to her family, Ahmed took advantage of her loyalty, choosing to live freely without the responsibilities of fatherhood and husbandry. Eventually, he abandoned her and their son, marrying another woman and depriving them of the emotional and financial support they deserved. Faced with this heartbreaking reality, Nivin knew she had to stand her ground, both for herself and her son. Determined not to let hardship define her, Nivin transformed this chapter of loss into one of empowerment. She immersed herself in study and self-reflection, developing her skills and understanding herself on a deeper level. Instead of letting the betrayal shape her, she turned her energy towards building a new life—one in which she would reclaim her self-worth and independence. With the odds stacked against her, she faced financial struggles, societal judgments, and jealousy from those who once surrounded her. Despite the challenges, she committed to building a life of dignity and strength, refusing to let herself fall under anyone's control again.

Through her beauty brand, Duchess Prestige, she channels her journey into a source of empowerment for women, encouraging them to find their inner strength and resilience. Her charity, honoring her son Sheikh Saeed bin Ahmed Al-

Maktoum, supports children with MBL immune deficiencies, furthering her legacy of compassion and advocacy. As an author, Duchess Nivin shares her wisdom in "*Peace, Please*", "A Star Mastering- The Feminine Enigma" and "*Mother's First Aid*", works dedicated to mental health, child protection, and resilience. As an Ambassador for Peace, she remains a beacon of hope, inspiring others to seek justice, peace, and respect.

Chapter 5

The Ten Secrets to Lasting Love

10 Secrets to Keep a Man's Love

The Secrets of Love: How to Keep and Deepen It

Ladies, many of you have often wondered, *"How can I make him love me?"* Winning a man's heart can be simple, but the real challenge, the one that makes love last, lies in a much more meaningful question: *How can I keep and deepen this love?*

Winning his heart is a wonderful first step, but don't fall into the trap of thinking that maintaining it will be easy! Love needs constant nurturing, even after you've won it. Keep him intrigued, a mystery he wants to solve every day. Remember: in love, there are no guarantees, only effort and connection.

1. Cultivate a Mystery and Keep His Heart Engaged

Winning his heart is only the beginning; the key to a lasting connection is to keep him intrigued and invested. Don't fall into a comfortable routine that removes all excitement. Instead, nurture a sense of curiosity in your relationship. Let him see that there are still parts of you he hasn't fully uncovered, dimensions of your personality that continue to unfold over time.

To do this, make space for both togetherness and independence. Pursue your own interests, maintain your passions, and dedicate time to your growth. When you're engaged with your own life, you bring new energy, stories, and insights into the relationship—things that keep him eager to learn more about you each day.

Keep the balance by sharing openly but leaving room for mystery. Show parts of yourself gradually, surprising him now and then with something unexpected, whether it's a new goal, a skill, or an idea that challenges his perspective. This subtle mystery creates anticipation, making him look forward to what's next. It's the art of staying fascinating while building depth, so he feels he's with someone dynamic—someone he'll want to keep discovering.

2. A Word of Wisdom on Distance

Love is an art of measured distance, a delicate balance between presence and absence. Come too close, and you risk smothering the spark of longing; drift too far, and the threads of memory may fray. To keep desire alive, tend to the fire with subtle, invisible gestures—let your influence be felt, not seen, like the quiet hand that stirs his soul yet never reveals itself. True passion endures in the mystery of this dance, in the space where two hearts remain bound yet free to yearn.

Make him feel that every 24 hours apart stretches into an eternity, each minute like a lifetime he aches to fill with you. Leave traces of yourself woven into his days— a word that lingers in his mind, a laugh that echoes in his silence, a fleeting image he catches as he closes his eyes. Keep a distance that invites his longing, yet offer small gestures to remind him that you're near, like a whisper he can't quite grasp. Let your absence be felt in ways that make him crave your presence, so that when you finally meet again, he feels the weight of every second spent without you, and nothing feels more precious.

3. Invite Him Into Your World

Love can feel especially intense for a woman because, more often than not, she is drawn first into the man's world—his habits, his routines, his spaces. But a true, lasting partnership flourishes when both lives intertwine, when each brings the other fully into their own world. Don't hold back from revealing your life to him. Show him what you're passionate about, the dreams that move you, the friends and spaces that shape who you are.

Invite him to experience what brings you joy, to see the things that spark your curiosity. Introduce him to the music, art, or ideas that inspire you, and let him witness the goals you work toward. This shared openness creates a balance, weaving both lives into one narrative where each finds richness in the other's world. Letting him into your life shows trust and depth; it allows the relationship to become

a true partnership, where both of you grow, both as individuals and as one.
For example, if you've joined him in watching football, why not invite him to something you love in return? You might find he's more open than you think.

Simple Ways to Bring Him Into Your World:

- Go grocery shopping together, even if it's just a quick errand.
- Cook a meal together, even if it's just a simple snack.
- Involve him with your family if he's serious about you, and introduce him to friends (without overdoing it) if you're still getting to know each other.
- Take walks together or try a workout session to stay close in a fun way.
- Make your space welcoming, a place he feels happy to spend time with you.

4. Make Small, Routine Changes for Lasting Interest

Every couple of weeks, make it a priority to break out of your usual routine by introducing something new—a fresh activity, a shared hobby, or even a small change to your everyday schedule. This could be anything from planning a quick weekend getaway to setting up an unexpected date night at a place you've never been. It might even be something simpler, like cooking a new recipe together or trying a creative class as a team. The key is to add a spark of novelty to your time together.

Shared new experiences, no matter how small, create a sense of adventure and deepen your connection. When you both step into unfamiliar territory, you're making memories, discovering new sides of each other, and adding layers to your relationship. These moments keep things exciting and remind both of you that there's always more to explore together, reinforcing your bond and keeping your connection fresh and dynamic. So whether it's a big adventure or a small change, make time for these shared firsts—they are the fuel that keeps the relationship lively and resilient.

5. Find Joy in Small Gestures

Often, it's the small, thoughtful gestures that create the deepest impact in a relationship. By consistently weaving little moments of kindness, joy, and warmth into his daily life, you show that you're invested in creating a lasting bond. These small acts, when practiced regularly, become a natural part of how you connect and can strengthen your relationship over time. Here's how to bring this into your relationship in a meaningful way:

Identify Simple Acts That Mean the Most: Start by paying attention to the little things that bring him happiness or comfort. These might be as simple as making his favorite coffee in the morning, sending an encouraging text during his day, or remembering something important to him. The key is not grand gestures but small, thoughtful actions that show you're attuned to him.

Be Consistent but Genuine: Make these small gestures part of your routine, so they come naturally. Leave notes, share a smile, listen without distractions, or celebrate his small wins. Over time, this consistency builds a foundation of warmth and reliability, letting him feel valued and cared for every day. It's not about making an effort to impress but rather showing that his happiness genuinely matters to you.

Stay Attentive and Evolve with His Needs: People's needs and preferences change, so remain attentive. As your relationship grows, your understanding of what comforts or inspires him will deepen. Adjust these small gestures as needed, always aiming to show that you're paying attention to him as he is now. This flexibility shows that your care is thoughtful and responsive rather than routine.

Allow It to Be a Natural Part of Your Bond: As you continue to show this care and warmth, these gestures will become a natural part of how you interact. When kindness becomes second nature, your relationship gains a steady rhythm of joy and connection, grounded in daily acts of affection.

Building a habit of small, thoughtful gestures isn't about grand displays but about maintaining a steady flow of warmth and attention. Over time, these actions create an environment of love and respect, where both of you feel secure and valued. They may seem like small things, but their impact can be lasting, helping to build a relationship that feels warm, supportive, and enduring.

6. Keep Some Mystery in the Routine

Routine can sometimes dull the spark in a relationship, but small, subtle surprises can reignite it and keep things exciting. By occasionally introducing a touch of spontaneity without making a big announcement, you create a sense of curiosity and anticipation. This keeps him intrigued and looking forward to what comes next, making each moment feel a little more special. Here's how to achieve this balance and keep the relationship fresh:

Incorporate Small, Unexpected Changes: Surprise doesn't have to mean anything drastic. Try a new hairstyle, wear a different style of clothing, or add a touch of something new to your usual look. Small shifts in appearance or style show that you're always evolving, which keeps his curiosity engaged. He'll notice these little changes and see that there's always something new to discover about you.

Create Shared New Experiences: Plan a day trip to a new spot, introduce him to a restaurant you've never tried, or suggest an activity you haven't done together. Don't announce it too far in advance—simply suggest it as an idea when the time feels right. These shared "firsts" add novelty and adventure to your relationship, creating fresh memories and keeping both of you engaged.

Surprise Him in Thoughtful, Gentle Ways: It's not about grand surprises but rather adding small twists to your routine that feel natural. Leave him a thoughtful note, send a playlist of songs that remind you of him, or bring home his favorite snack unexpectedly. These little touches show that you're thinking of him and that you value making the ordinary feel special.

Stay Unpredictable, Yet Genuine: The goal is to keep things interesting without forcing anything that feels unnatural. Let the surprises be small enough to feel genuine, but noticeable enough to catch his attention. The combination of familiarity with a touch of the unexpected creates a dynamic energy that helps prevent the relationship from falling into monotony.

Balance Surprises with Consistency: While surprises can bring excitement, they work best alongside a strong foundation of consistency and trust. When he knows he can rely on you but also expect occasional bursts of spontaneity, it creates a perfect blend of stability and intrigue.

By mixing things up in small, thoughtful ways, you're adding layers of excitement and freshness to the relationship. These subtle surprises, spread out over time, keep him engaged and looking forward to what's next.

This approach allows the relationship to grow naturally while preserving an element of mystery, making each moment together feel both comfortable and new.

7. Don't Be Afraid to Lead

Sometimes, he'll enjoy taking the lead, but it can be equally refreshing for him to experience things on your terms, guided by your energy and ideas. To keep things balanced and exciting, let him step into your world in a way that feels natural to him, where he feels he's actively involved in deciding what comes next. Whether it's planning a new kind of date or introducing an activity you both haven't tried, invite him to follow your lead without it feeling like you're taking full control. Here's how to create this dynamic in a way that makes him feel empowered and involved:

Present Ideas as Options for Him to Choose From:

Instead of planning everything directly, casually suggest a couple of options or ideas, then ask what he thinks. For instance, you might say, "I was thinking about trying out this cool art class or maybe going on a scenic hike this weekend—what do you think?" This approach lets him feel he's choosing the activity while you guide the direction with your interests.

Express Enthusiasm for Shared Experiences:

When suggesting something new, focus on the enjoyment and discovery you'll both get from it. Say things like, "I'd love to see what you think about this spot I found" or "I thought it would be fun to do something different together." This way, he senses that it's a collaborative experience rather than you simply leading. Your enthusiasm makes him feel included and lets him take part in bringing the idea to life.

Allow Space for His Input and Ideas: After suggesting an activity, invite his feedback and listen to his thoughts on how to approach it. Let him offer ideas on timing, details, or variations. For example, if you mention going to a new restaurant, you could ask if he has any thoughts on what to order or if he'd like to decide where you'll go afterward. This shows that while you're bringing something new to the table, he's involved in shaping the experience.

Show Genuine Curiosity About His Reaction: Once you're in the experience, express interest in how he's enjoying it. Simple comments like, "I'm glad we tried this—what do you think?" let him feel valued and recognized, showing that you're leading with a desire to share something together rather than pushing him into your world.

Subtly Encourage Him to Take the Lead Midway: As the activity unfolds, let him take charge in small ways. For example, if you're exploring a new city, encourage him to choose which spots to visit next. This gives him the chance to feel like an active decision-maker, reinforcing that his role is integral to the experience.

By using this approach, you're inviting him into your world without taking over his sense of control. He'll feel involved and valued, enjoying the experience as if he's chosen it himself, while still appreciating the new perspectives you bring. This balance of gentle guidance and mutual involvement fosters a deeper connection and keeps the relationship dynamic, allowing each of you to enjoy leading and exploring together.

8. Avoid Broadcasting Your Changes

Change within a relationship can be delicate and even risky, as sudden shifts can create tension or distance. Announcing that you're changing or focusing too much on it can feel abrupt and unsettling for a partner, sometimes leading to misunderstandings or even a break in the connection. Instead, approach any personal growth or adjustments thoughtfully and gradually, allowing your actions to speak for themselves. This careful, balanced approach shows that you're evolving without threatening the relationship's stability. Here's how to navigate this wisely:

Make Small, Gradual Changes: Rather than diving into big changes all at once, start with small adjustments that reflect your growth. Whether you're adopting a new habit, pursuing a passion, or improving a skill, begin slowly and let the changes blend into your everyday life. This way, he can get used to the new aspects of you without feeling a sudden shift that disrupts the relationship.

Communicate Openly and Reassure Him: While you don't need to announce every change, let him know you're committed to the relationship as you grow. For instance, if you're focused on self-improvement, mention how your goals contribute positively to both your lives rather than distancing yourself from him. A comment like, "I've been working on becoming a better version of myself, and I'm excited for us to grow together," reassures him that your growth benefits the relationship.

Involve Him Subtly in Your Growth: Invite him to share in certain aspects of your journey without directly asking him to change. For example, if you're adopting a healthier lifestyle, suggest trying a new recipe together or invite him on a weekend hike. When he sees how your positive changes make you happier or more engaged, he may naturally feel inspired to join you without feeling pressured.

Stay Grounded in the Relationship: Remain consistent in the relationship areas that matter most, so he doesn't feel you're pulling away. Make time for shared interests, traditions, and quality moments together. Let him see that, while you're growing, your commitment to him remains steady. This helps him feel secure, knowing that your personal evolution doesn't mean a loss of connection.

Allow Him Space for His Own Growth: When you're changing, he may feel the need to evolve too, or he may resist initially. Give him space to adjust to the new dynamic, offering support without pressure. By respecting his pace, you build an environment where both of you can grow individually while keeping the relationship aligned.

Be Patient and Observant: Change takes time, and so does adaptation within a relationship. Pay attention to his responses, ensuring he feels comfortable. If he seems distant or uneasy, approach the topic with empathy. Understanding his reactions allows you to adapt your pace, finding a balance that keeps the relationship strong.

By taking a careful, thoughtful approach to change, you allow room for growth without causing unnecessary disruption. He'll notice the positive shifts over time, and if the process is gradual and considerate, he's more likely to accept and even embrace your evolution. This approach helps protect the relationship's harmony, allowing both of you to grow together naturally.

9. Embrace Newness Together

Continue exploring new experiences together, even after years in the relationship. These shared adventures create cherished memories and bring excitement to everyday life, keeping the relationship vibrant and engaging. The joy of discovering something new together brings you closer, reminding you that there's always more to explore with each other. As the saying goes, "There's always a first time for everything!"—and these moments of novelty can become the highlights of your time together. Here's how to embrace this approach and the pleasure it brings:

Choose Experiences That Reflect Shared Interests: Start with activities you both find intriguing—whether it's taking a cooking class, exploring a nearby town, trying out a new sport, or learning a language. Sharing something that excites you both deepens your connection and makes the experience more enjoyable. As you learn and navigate these new moments together, you're building memories that strengthen the bond you share.

Enjoy the Discovery Together: The beauty of trying something new as a couple lies in the discovery process. When you're both out of your comfort zones, it's easier to feel open, playful, and vulnerable. Laughing over new challenges, cheering each other on, and celebrating small successes bring lightness and joy into the relationship. These moments remind you of the adventure that first drew you together and keep that spark alive.

Plan Spontaneous Adventures: Routine can sometimes make life feel predictable, so break it up with spontaneous plans. Pack a bag for an unplanned road trip, take an afternoon for a surprise picnic, or suggest a quick detour to somewhere neither of you has been before. These little adventures add a layer of excitement and anticipation to your days, giving both of you something to look forward to.

Create Traditions of Exploration: Establish a habit of trying something new regularly, perhaps once a month or every few weeks. It could be as simple as picking a new restaurant or as big as planning an annual getaway to an unexplored destination. This tradition of exploration keeps your relationship fresh and brings shared anticipation for what's to come.

Appreciate the Memories You Make Together: Reflecting on the experiences you share builds gratitude for your journey together. Capture photos, create small mementos, or make it a ritual to revisit your favorite moments. Each memory serves as a reminder of the joy you find together, adding richness and depth to your relationship.

Trying new things together brings a sense of adventure and growth, helping to keep the relationship lively and meaningful. The shared memories you build become treasured parts of your story as a couple, creating a foundation of joy, laughter, and mutual discovery that only grows deeper over time. By keeping this sense of exploration alive, you continue to evolve together, always finding new reasons to appreciate one another.

10. Create a Balanced Love Between Familiarity and Mystery

Cherish each day as an opportunity to create a unique connection with him, blending the comfort of familiarity with the spark of curiosity. A truly deep relationship thrives on balance—make him feel secure and valued, but leave room for a hint of mystery, keeping love lively and evolving. A lasting connection combines closeness with a healthy sense of independence, creating a dynamic relationship that's both fulfilling and exciting.

How to achieve this balance in a way that makes love stay vibrant and strong

Cultivate Daily Moments of Warmth and Appreciation: Show your love consistently in small ways, whether it's through a heartfelt compliment, a small gesture of kindness, or simply being present and attentive. This day-to-day warmth builds a foundation of trust and security, making him feel cherished and appreciated. As he feels secure in your connection, it allows room for excitement and spontaneity without fear of losing stability.

Introduce Gentle Surprises: Keep a touch of unpredictability alive with small, thoughtful surprises. This could be as simple as trying a new recipe for dinner, planning a spontaneous date night, or leaving him a note expressing how much he means to you. These surprises don't need to be extravagant; their purpose is to show that you're still actively invested in the relationship and that you value keeping things fresh and engaging.

Maintain Your Individual Interests and Passions: Independence is key to keeping a relationship dynamic. Pursue your hobbies, career goals, and friendships outside of the relationship. When you bring your own experiences, stories, and achievements back to him, you add richness to the connection. This independence keeps you interesting and allows both of you to grow, creating a partnership that's both close-knit and inspiring.

Stay Curious About Each Other: Even after years together, continue to ask questions, listen deeply, and learn new things about each other. People evolve over time, and showing curiosity about his thoughts, dreams, and goals allows you to deepen your understanding of him as he changes. This curiosity strengthens your emotional connection and keeps both of you engaged.

Balance Stability with Flexibility: While consistency is comforting, flexibility is equally important. Be open to adapting your routines, especially as life changes. Allow room for spontaneity in your plans, and let the relationship evolve naturally without feeling like everything needs to follow a set path. This adaptability keeps love resilient and ready for whatever comes next.

By blending consistency with a touch of the unexpected, you create a relationship that's both steady and full of life. Love thrives on a combination of commitment and playfulness, allowing you to grow together while keeping a sense of curiosity and excitement alive. Embrace the journey with intention and openness, knowing that the balance of security and spontaneity is what makes love last, giving you both a powerful connection that deepens over time.

Understanding him

To build a deeply fulfilling relationship, start by truly understanding his personality, his past experiences, and the cultural background that shapes him. This awareness shows that you respect his identity, honoring both his strengths and his vulnerabilities. But respect doesn't mean losing yourself or reshaping your life entirely around him; instead, it means finding ways to support each other's growth while keeping your individual identities intact.

Here's how to do it in a way that lets both of you flourish:

1. **Learn and Respect, Without Losing Yourself:** Take time to understand his values, his personal boundaries, and his history. Show genuine interest in

his culture, traditions, and viewpoints, but don't feel pressured to adopt everything he believes or lives by. Celebrate the differences, and approach his world with curiosity, knowing that his experiences enrich the relationship. Likewise, invite him into your world by sharing your culture, values, and passions. This way, both of you bring something unique to the relationship, creating a mutual exchange rather than one side absorbing the other.

2. **Maintain Your Identity and Boundaries:** Keep the parts of your life that are meaningful to you—your work, friendships, hobbies, and goals. Being passionate about your own life makes you interesting and shows him that your world is valuable. Make it clear that you won't give up these aspects, and encourage him to do the same. By respecting each other's individuality, you each bring fresh experiences and perspectives into the relationship, which keeps the connection vibrant and evolving.

3. **Communicate Your Needs and Set Boundaries:** Define clear boundaries together so that both of you feel respected. If there's something important to you, like a career aspiration or a weekly time with friends, discuss it openly. When he understands that your work, social life, or personal growth matters, he's more likely to respect those aspects of your life. This boundary-setting goes both ways: listen to his needs and support his individuality too. Boundaries allow both of you to feel secure, supported, and respected,

without either person feeling overrun or compromised.

4. **Show Support Without Losing Dignity:** To be a supportive partner, listen to his ideas and respect his opinions, but don't shy away from sharing your own thoughts, beliefs, or solutions. Offer constructive perspectives when needed and avoid criticism or overstepping. Your insights and independent opinions will make him value you as a partner who is strong and capable, someone who brings wisdom and understanding into his life rather than simply agreeing with everything.

5. **Encourage Growth Together:** See yourselves as a team—two people growing together, each bringing unique qualities and experiences that enrich the other. Foster shared goals, but let there be space for personal growth too. By being open, respectful, and encouraging, you each gain a partner who truly values and supports the other's journey.

Maintaining this balance between closeness and individuality allows both of you to feel secure and valued. In the process, you're building a relationship where he sees you as a partner he admires and respects—a person whose presence is valuable precisely because you bring your whole self to the relationship.

Routine: The Silent Threat to Relationships

Routine can be the quiet burial ground of passion. For those who embrace growth and change, it's easy to see how habits can become traps. But for anyone who resists stretching their thinking or who fears change, routine can feel almost insurmountable—a comfort zone that quickly becomes a cage. When we stop evolving, relationships often become dull, predictable, and even obligatory. It's natural to feel this way from time to time, but there are ways to rekindle the excitement and keep your relationship fresh.

How to Stand Out and Keep Things Interesting

If you sense a spark fading in your relationship, here are a few ways to reintroduce excitement:

1. **Create a Sense of Distance:** Give each other some breathing room. Spend time with positive, vibrant friends who bring out your love for life. When your partner sees you thriving and enjoying yourself, it creates a healthy sense of admiration and a desire to reconnect.

2. **Limit Calls Gradually:** Reduce your calls slightly to give each other a bit of space. When you do speak, keep the conversation sweet and positive. If he asks, "Where have you been?" you can simply reply, "Oh, just catching up on things." This keeps the mood light and prevents any feelings of obligation.

3. **Be Present, but Not Overly Available:** It's okay to make him miss you. Give him the chance to reach out and notice your absence. This doesn't mean anything is wrong; it's just a gentle reminder of your independence, which can actually reignite his interest.

What to Avoid Asking When Things Feel Unstable

During uncertain times, avoid asking questions that create pressure or hint at insecurity, like:

- "Is something wrong?"
- "Do you still feel the same way about me?"
- "Are you upset with me?"

These questions can make a man feel cornered, especially if he's already in a reflective state. Instead, focus on maintaining your own sense of joy and fulfillment. Men often sense neediness and, paradoxically, pull back even more when they feel it. So, be mindful of holding onto your individuality. If he senses that you're secure and content, he'll often come around and re-engage naturally.

Remember, keeping a relationship strong means staying attuned to each other while allowing for growth and independence. Give him space to miss you, and you'll both keep the excitement alive.

This version focuses on encouraging a balanced approach, highlighting the importance of space and independence in maintaining a healthy relationship. Let me know if you'd like to explore other angles or add specific tips!

Protecting Your Relationship: How to Keep Your Partner's Affection and Guard Against Temptation

Relationship dynamics, and strategies for keeping your bond secure.

Relationships face unique challenges today, with temptations and distractions often just a click away. Yet, a healthy, trusting relationship can be the strongest defense against these outside pressures. Some people might not respect the boundaries of a committed relationship and might even pursue someone who is already in a partnership. In these cases, it's easy to feel anxious or uncertain, but there are positive steps you can take to strengthen your bond and keep it resilient against external influences.

In this guide, we'll explore why some people pursue those who are in relationships, how to build a bond that naturally deflects outside temptations, and specific strategies to maintain a happy, secure relationship with your partner.

Understanding Why Some People Don't Respect Boundaries

1. Motivations Behind Pursuing Committed People

While it's natural to feel threatened by someone else's interest in your partner, understanding the motivations behind this behavior can help put things in perspective. Often, people pursue those in relationships for the thrill or challenge. The "forbidden" element can make a committed person seem more attractive, sparking interest simply because they are "off-limits." For some, it's about validation or seeking attention rather than a true connection.

2. Recognizing Red Flags

If you notice that someone is spending too much time with your partner, messaging them frequently, or crossing personal boundaries, it's worth addressing calmly with your partner. Red flags might include:

- Unusual frequency in communication.
- Signs of excessive admiration or compliments.
- Attempts to isolate your partner from their normal friend group.

Approach these situations by calmly discussing your feelings without accusing your partner. It's important to remember that your relationship is built on trust, and open communication is crucial to keep that trust intact.

Strengthening Your Bond with Your Partner

1. Prioritizing Honest Communication

Open communication is the foundation of any strong relationship. It builds trust and shows both partners that they're on the same team. Make it a habit to share your feelings openly, and encourage your partner to do the same. Discussing boundaries and establishing mutual respect creates an unspoken understanding that discourages others from getting too close.

Sample Conversation Tip: Instead of saying, "I'm worried about you talking to her," try, "I feel most connected when we can be open with each other about what's on our minds. I want us to always have that trust."

2. Building Trust and Confidence in Each Other

Trust can be one of the most attractive qualities in a relationship. If your partner knows that you believe in them and their integrity, it builds a sense of mutual respect. Trust allows both partners to feel valued, appreciated, and secure in each other's loyalty.

Encourage each other's independence and personal growth. This not only brings a positive energy into the relationship but also prevents any sense of "ownership" that could otherwise become suffocating. By building trust and celebrating each other's individuality, you naturally protect your relationship from external threats.

3. Keeping the Relationship Dynamic and Exciting

Routine is a common relationship challenge, but a bit of effort can make a big difference. Look for ways to bring novelty into your relationship, even with small gestures. Surprises, spontaneous adventures, or even cooking a new dish together can reignite excitement and keep things fresh.

Example Idea: Try a "bucket list" date night, where each of you writes down five things you'd love to do together. Pick one each month to keep things lively and give you both something to look forward to.

How to "Win" Your Partner's Heart Every Day

1. Embrace Your Independence

One of the most attractive qualities in a relationship is independence. By pursuing your own interests, hobbies, and friendships, you cultivate your happiness and make yourself more intriguing. When your partner sees you thriving and enjoying life, it reminds them of why they were drawn to you in the first place. Independence also helps balance the relationship, showing that while you deeply care for your partner, you also value your own growth.

2. Show Appreciation and Gratitude

Small acts of appreciation go a long way in nurturing a relationship. Thanking your partner for the little things, offering genuine compliments, and recognizing their efforts reinforce the positive aspects of your bond. These small gestures may seem minor, but they create a lasting impression and help your partner feel loved and valued.

Sample Phrase: "Thank you for always making time for us, even when you're busy. I feel lucky to have you."

3. Setting Boundaries Together

Boundaries are essential in any healthy relationship. Have open discussions about what you both consider appropriate interactions with friends or acquaintances of the opposite gender. Setting these boundaries together fosters respect and removes any potential misunderstandings. This way, you both know each other's comfort zones, which can prevent issues before they arise.

Recognizing and Deflecting the Influence of a "Dangerous" Third Party

1. Avoid Jealousy and Insecurity

Reacting to outside interest with jealousy or insecurity can unintentionally push your partner away. Instead, approach situations with calmness and confidence. Trust that your partner values your relationship, and avoid letting external influences make you doubt each other. If you're feeling insecure, talk to your partner about it without framing it as an accusation.

2. Promoting Open Communication When You Notice Concerns

If you sense that someone is becoming overly interested in your partner, address it directly but respectfully. Calmly explain how certain behaviors make you feel and suggest ways to set healthy boundaries without pressuring your partner. It's important to keep the tone of these conversations positive and supportive, so your partner doesn't feel accused but rather feels empowered to keep the relationship strong.

Sample Phrase: "I trust you completely, but I just want to be open about something that's been on my mind. Let's make sure we're both comfortable with how we interact with others."

3. Fostering Positivity Rather than Pressure

When dealing with an outside interest, focus on positivity instead of pressure. Being overly clingy or demanding can create tension. Instead, remain confident and happy in the relationship, knowing that a calm, respectful approach will leave a lasting impact. Positivity draws your partner closer, while excessive pressure can have the opposite effect.

Example Strategy: When your partner is spending time with friends, give them space but make plans for when they return. This balance helps your partner feel free and valued.

The Power of Confidence and Self-Worth

1. Cultivating Confidence

Confidence is a magnetic quality in any relationship. When you feel secure in yourself, it not only boosts your self-esteem but also shows your partner that you're self-assured. Confident individuals are often happier, more resilient, and more attractive in their relationships.

2. Practicing Self-Care

Maintaining your own well-being—physically, emotionally, and mentally—helps you bring your best self to the relationship. Self-care keeps you balanced and fulfilled, which in turn positively influences your connection with your partner. When both partners feel happy and whole, it strengthens the bond and makes outside threats less impactful.

Subtle Transformations in Appearance

The essence of keeping romance alive and excitement flourishing in a relationship is embracing change, spontaneity, and a sense of adventure. Routine can easily settle into every part of life, including the way we present ourselves and interact with our partners.
Small changes in your style can make a significant impact. Change your hairstyle, try a new makeup look, or switch up your wardrobe occasionally. This keeps things fresh and maintains a sense of intrigue without losing your core identity. For example, if he admires your natural hair color, surprise him by trying a different shade or styling it differently.

Balance of Stability and Surprise in Behaviour

Cultivate different facets of yourself: be his confidante, his cheerleader, his calming presence, and occasionally the spark that challenges him. Embrace being playful, gentle, wise, and bold at different times. It's about showing him that you're multifaceted, someone he can continuously learn more about

Keeping Romance Alive Through Subtle Change

In a lasting relationship, romance and excitement are fuelled by embracing small changes, a sense of adventure, and balance between stability and surprise. Routine can settle in over time, but subtle transformations can keep things fresh and intriguing.

1. **Refreshing Your Style**
   Small changes in appearance can spark a sense of renewal. Try a new hairstyle, makeup look, or wardrobe update. These shifts keep things exciting, creating a sense of novelty while preserving your core identity. If he loves your natural look, perhaps surprise him with a different style, adding an element of intrigue without losing your essence.
2. **Showing Multifaceted Sides of Yourself**
   Be a confidante, cheerleader, and calming presence, but also let yourself be playful, bold, and spontaneous. Displaying different aspects of who you are keeps your connection vibrant and ever-evolving.
3. **Adding Small Changes to Daily Life**
   Incorporate small, memorable moments into your routine. A new perfume, an unexpected gesture, or a cozy, picnic-style evening at home can break up the monotony and create lasting memories.

4. **Balancing Planning and Spontaneity**
   Combine planned moments with spur-of-the-moment adventures. Suggest a quick getaway or an impromptu date, and mix it with relaxed nights in. This balance of spontaneity and calm fosters a dynamic where there's always something new to discover.
5. **Keeping Things Light and Playful**
   Humour and playfulness can deepen your bond. Make him laugh, share teasing moments, and create shared, joyful experiences that make your connection both fun and memorable.
6. **Blending Boldness with Elegance**
   Embrace sophistication for formal occasions and a laid-back vibe for casual adventures, showing you can thrive in all aspects of life and inviting him to join you on that journey.
7. **Staying Authentic**
   While change is refreshing, stay true to yourself. Introduce new facets gradually and with authenticity—maintaining a sense of mystery and depth that allows your partner to keep discovering new things about you.

Nicole's Journey of Growth to Win Albert Back

Nicole had deeply loved Albert, but over time, they drifted apart. When she learned he'd married someone else, she felt heartbroken yet resolute. Rather than retreat, she took a reflective journey inward, resolving to become her best self without manipulation, focusing instead on genuine personal growth. Her path was marked by self-reflection, subtle gestures of kindness, and a renewed embrace of her passions.

1. **Self-Reflection and Acceptance**
   Nicole spent time reflecting on their relationship, realising how small moments of complacency had added up. She accepted her mistakes and committed to growth, becoming a stronger version of herself who could respect Albert's choices and cherish a possible future.
2. **Offering Steady Friendship**
   Despite her heartbreak, she stayed a respectful, constant friend in Albert's life. She offered support in his times of need without expectation, demonstrating a love that sought his happiness above her own desires.
3. **Small Acts of Kindness**
   When Albert's mother fell ill, Nicole offered quiet support, coordinating care with family members. Her selflessness moved Albert, reminding him of the warmth and strength she had once brought into his life.
4. **Rediscovering Passions**
   Nicole explored photography, a shared passion from their past, finding joy in capturing meaningful moments. Albert noticed her work online, and they began a friendly, lighthearted exchange, rekindling a connection rooted in shared interests.

5. **Attending a Shared Event**
When Albert invited her to an exhibition, Nicole attended with no expectations. They laughed, reminisced, and shared a deep connection. Though she respected his current relationship, her presence reminded him of the bond they once shared.
6. **Living Authentically**
Nicole continued pursuing her dreams and building a life full of joy, sharing occasional updates with Albert. He saw her bloom independently, making him question if he had ever fully appreciated her depth.
7. **A Confession from the Heart**
Eventually, Albert reached out to Nicole, expressing doubts about his marriage. She listened without judgment and confessed her enduring feelings, while still respecting his commitment and giving him space to decide.
8. **Giving Him Space**
After their heart-to-heart, Nicole withdrew slightly, allowing Albert the freedom to reflect. True love, she believed, couldn't be rushed. Over time, he recognized the depth and authenticity of her love—a stark contrast to his current relationship.
9. **A Reunion Built on Growth**
In time, Albert chose to end his marriage, seeking a second chance with Nicole. At first, she hesitated, unwilling to be a rebound. But as he demonstrated his own growth, they

began to rebuild trust. Their love story came full circle, redefined by maturity, patience, and mutual respect.

Examples of Meaningful Actions

To help bring Nicole's story to life, here are actions she might take to convey her growth and dedication:

- **Personal Transformation:** Nicole embraces qualities Albert loved about her—kindness, spirit, ambition—showing that she's still the person he fell in love with, but now more grounded and self-aware.
- **Thoughtful Gesture:** She might create a scrapbook of their memories, with personal notes that express her gratitude for their shared experiences, reminding him of the depth of her affection.
- **Revisiting Special Places:** A surprise visit to a significant place from their past could help them reconnect, tapping into shared history and nostalgia.
- **Heartfelt Letter:** Nicole could write a letter acknowledging her mistakes and expressing her growth and commitment, demonstrating sincerity and vulnerability.
- **Shared Adventure:** A spontaneous outing that aligns with his interests could create new memories, showing her willingness to step into his world and rekindle excitement.

- **Being Present:** Nicole might show up to support Albert during important events, proving that her investment in his happiness transcends romance.
- **Owning Past Mistakes:** By directly apologising for specific actions, she conveys understanding and sincerity, paving the way for forgiveness.
- **Learning Something New:** She could embrace one of Albert's hobbies, showing interest in the things he loves as a way to reconnect on a deeper level.
- **Everyday Acts of Kindness:** Small, consistent gestures of affection and patience could gradually build a sense of closeness, reestablishing trust over time.
- **Setting Future Plans:** As they grow closer, suggesting a shared project or adventure might foster a new sense of anticipation and partnership.

Through these gestures, Nicole's actions reflect genuine growth and enduring love, offering Albert a glimpse of the deeply fulfilling relationship they could have. Their journey shows how patience, authenticity, and personal evolution can lead to a love that's both lasting and enriched by the trials they've overcome.

This revised narrative streamlines the story while emphasising Nicole's inner transformation and the powerful impact of small, thoughtful gestures. It conveys a love story rooted in personal growth and resilience, showing how meaningful reconnection can flourish through authenticity and patience.

The Difference between Kind Women and Wild Women

Imagine this: a woman finds herself drawn to a man unlike any she's ever known. He's adventurous, lives on his own terms, and embraces a life that's spontaneous and unpredictable. He doesn't care about fitting in; instead, he's focused on experiencing life fully with those he truly cares about. This shift from the familiar awakens something within her, making her feel exhilarated, as if she's left behind the monotony of her life.

The Kind Nurturer and the Wild Lover

To many men, there's often no middle ground in how they see a woman: she's either the "nurturer" or the "lover." And these two roles couldn't be more different. A lover, unlike a nurturer, captivates him, keeps him on his toes, and sparks a feeling of unpredictability he finds addictive. She's spontaneous, a bit mischievous, and brings out his playful side. She cares for herself as much as, if not more than, she cares for him, creating a sense of independence that he finds irresistible. His friends may tease him, calling him "soft" or "wrapped around her finger," but he's too enchanted to care.

She doesn't focus on caretaking or "mothering"; instead, she fills his life with excitement and joy.

On the other hand, the "nurturer" adopts a more maternal role. Her care is constant and can border on smothering. She worries about him as if he were her child, always managing his needs, planning for him, and creating a sense of comfort that, while safe, lacks the thrill he craves. Financially, he may even rely on her, and he feels no pressure to impress her. Life with her becomes routine, predictable, and, at times, uninspiring. Though he respects her, he often feels weighed down, like a dependent rather than a partner.

In this story, meet Emma and Jake. Emma is the embodiment of kindness, striving to be perfect in every aspect of life, especially in her relationship. She takes on the ideal nurturing role, always caring, planning, and sacrificing her true self to meet societal expectations. Jake, on the other hand, is spontaneous and free-spirited, driven by a love for adventure and discovery. Emma's focus is on keeping everything stable, urging Jake to "settle down" and "take things seriously." To her, a strong relationship means predictability and consistency.

But as much as Jake respects Emma, he starts to feel like he's living under a motherly gaze. She plans his meals, checks on his medications, and makes sure he's well cared for, even though he doesn't need it to that extent. He appreciates her kindness, but it starts to feel more like nurturing than a romantic partnership. Emma wants to help him become his best self in her eyes, but in doing so, she loses the opportunity to connect with him as a true partner rather than his caretaker.

Then, Jake meets Mia, a vivacious, unpredictable woman at a social gathering. From the moment they start talking, he feels a spark he can't ignore. Mia brings an easy, joyful energy into his life, offering him a new perspective. She's light-hearted, independent, and knows how to balance her freedom with their connection. She joins him in his adventures, but she's not always there, which makes him miss her and crave her presence even more.

Unlike Emma, who desires constant closeness, Mia gives Jake space to breathe, leaving him wanting more. She doesn't try to control him or shape his decisions; instead, she simply enjoys their time together without expecting anything in return. Their conversations flow effortlessly, their chemistry is undeniable, and their connection is electric. When his friends tease him about being "under her spell," he wears it like a badge of honour.

When people ask him why he loves Mia, he can't quite put it into words. There's no list, no reason – just a magnetic, almost inexplicable connection. But when asked why he respects Emma, he can detail her many caring, responsible qualities. Deep down, Jake knows that while Emma's kindness and steadiness are qualities anyone would admire, his heart is drawn to Mia, the woman who makes him feel truly alive, challenged, and free.

In the end, Jake realises he admires Emma but adores Mia – the difference between a kind nurturer and a wild lover.

To survive, you have to master the art of ignoring professionally.

To live peacefully in a relationship, it's essential to master the art of selective ignoring. Ignoring can be a blessing, yet many overlook its value. Often, after years together, some people think that digging deeper into every detail, asking endless questions, or searching for hidden information will strengthen the bond. But there's a difference between knowing your partner's character and intruding on their private matters. Knowing who you're with is essential, of course, but there's no need to overstep into spaces that only lead to frustration or insecurity.

For example, if your partner mentions someone from their past, it might spark curiosity. But pressing too hard to know every detail—especially if you discover that person is attractive—can create insecurities that may have never existed. Often, these little bits of information plant seeds of doubt, making you imagine scenarios and worry needlessly, while your partner remains oblivious.

Here's a common pitfall: some women feel compelled to check their partner's phone. But ask yourself—what are you hoping to find? Each person has private exchanges with friends that may seem silly or out of context but mean little.

They aren't necessarily betrayals or secrets—just harmless conversations.

Take the example of Martha and Khalid, who have been married for seven years. Khalid, a devoted husband, has eyes only for Martha. Yet, Martha's constant suspicion leads her to check his phone repeatedly, searching for something that isn't there. One day, she reads a conversation between Khalid and his friends that was simply lighthearted banter, but she misinterprets it and feels hurt. This constant need to find reassurance ultimately damages her self-confidence, strains the relationship, and shifts the dynamic.

We asked men about their thoughts on women who routinely intrude on their privacy, and here's what they said:

- 80% felt it shows insecurity
- 62% said it makes them feel like they aren't in control of the relationship
- 35% noted that their love diminishes
- 74% said their jealousy decreases
- 42% said they lose respect for their partner
- 87% felt trust is lacking
- 44% admitted they distance themselves as a result

The message is clear. Men highly value their sense of privacy; it's a space they feel is their own. If it's encroached upon, both partners end up frustrated, and there's a real risk of driving him away instead of pulling him closer.

In relationships, ignoring certain details is genuinely an art—one that brings inner peace. By focusing on yourself and your personal growth, you naturally encourage your partner's interest and respect. So, next time you feel tempted to pry, remember: cultivating your own sense of self will make you both happier and healthier as a couple.

Laughter, playfulness, seriousness, and love

Imagine you're in a wonderful relationship with someone, and everything seems perfect. But suddenly, you feel that he's become distant, or maybe he's spending more time with his friends. What would you do? Wait—don't answer, because we already know! You'd simply bring it up to him.

You'd say, feeling all hurt, "Why do you hang out with your friends more than me??" Hold up! Stop and listen. If you're already happy with your life and mention it to him in a lighthearted, joking way, then fine. But if you're truly sad and frustrated? Come on, really? Follow these few steps, and you'll see your life change. But don't just try them for a day or two, then give up if he doesn't respond right away. That just means you lack patience, and you won't get what you want as long as you're like that! Life itself is a game, and relationships are a part of that game. Relationships are never just pure stability and prosperity, and anyone who says otherwise has missed the point.

Think about it. If you see life as just stability with a partner, that's a sign he's only with her to keep the peace. The real adventure, the thrill, and the joy are with someone he genuinely loves being around. A relationship is like the stock market—it goes up and down. And that's normal; everyone experiences it. When you see that your "stocks" with him have dropped, only then should you change things up.

Don't be sensitive and read into it if a guy wants time with his friends; it's not that deep. Men are simple and often look for two main things: fun and good food. When he finds fun with you, do you really think he'd choose his friends over you all the time? No way! He'll see his friends, but he'll keep an eye on the clock, eager to get back to you, text you, or meet you. But if you're always sad or needy when he's around, he may be there physically, but his heart and mind are somewhere else.

Why is he pulling away? Only he knows. But you should be able to tell if he's seeking out friends, another girl, or even a hobby to escape from you.

Take Ryan, for example—one of the most charming and mischievous men around. Every day, he'd meet a new girl—no, correction, four girls in a single day! And you'd never see him with the same girl twice. Ryan was, to everyone, a bit like a rockstar. Every girl he met would become attached within an hour. He met Sarah, and she had a simple quality that caught his attention. Unlike the other girls, who became wildly jealous and tried to change him, Sarah was confident and never tried to control him. She'd say, "Go out and have fun with your friends, I'm meeting up with mine." So when Ryan was out with his friends, he didn't think about the many girls who wanted his attention; instead, he thought about his next move. Sarah's confidence made her different.

So, next time you're tempted to complain, think about how confidence and independence could turn things around for you.

Chapter 6

Understanding the Zodiac Signs – Chakras

Understanding the Zodiac Signs and Their Influence in Relationships

The zodiac offers a fascinating lens through which to view relationship dynamics, shedding light on the diverse ways each sign approaches love and connection. By understanding the astrological influences on yourself and your partner, you can gain a deeper appreciation for the strengths, challenges, and potential of your relationship. Remember, astrology serves as a guide, not a rulebook, and the most successful relationships are built on mutual understanding, respect, and a willingness to grow together.

In the world of astrology, zodiac signs are often thought of as guiding lights, offering insights into personality, compatibility, and even relationship dynamics. Each sign, from fiery Aries to mystical Pisces, carries unique traits that shape how individuals express themselves, approach love, and connect with others. In this chapter, we'll delve into the characteristics of each zodiac sign and explore how these qualities influence romantic relationships. By understanding the essence of each sign, you can gain insights into both your own behaviors and those of your partner, allowing for deeper connections and more fulfilling partnerships.

Introduction: The Power of Star Signs, Chakras, and Spiritual Protection

In a world where personal growth, self-awareness, and meaningful relationships are valued more than ever, many people are turning to the wisdom of ancient practices to better understand themselves and protect their energy. Two powerful frameworks—the zodiac and the chakra system—offer guidance in understanding the complex interplay between personality, emotional needs, and spiritual energy. By learning how to harness the insights of these systems, you can achieve deeper clarity about yourself and your relationships, while also building energetic resilience.

The zodiac, or astrology, categorizes each of us under one of twelve star signs, each ruled by specific elements and planets that shape our core traits and how we interact with others. These signs reveal our strengths, weaknesses, and how we approach relationships, helping us navigate both self-discovery and compatibility with others. Understanding your own star sign, as well as those of your loved ones, offers valuable insights into behaviors, motivations, and what you need to feel fulfilled.

Complementing the zodiac is the chakra system, an ancient concept from Eastern philosophy that describes the seven primary energy centers in the body. Each chakra corresponds to specific physical, emotional, and spiritual qualities. By understanding the chakra system, you can recognize and balance the energies that influence everything from self-confidence and communication to love and intuition. When balanced, chakras allow us to live harmoniously; when blocked or overactive, they can lead to physical ailments, emotional imbalances, and relationship challenges.

Finally, as you explore these tools for growth, it is also essential to understand and practice energetic protection. Just as we have physical boundaries, we also have an energy field, or aura, that can absorb negativity or become depleted by daily stressors. Spiritual protection techniques such as grounding, visualization, and energy cleansing can help you maintain strong personal boundaries and keep your energy aligned, shielding you from influences that do not serve your highest good.

Together, these practices—astrology, chakra work, and spiritual protection—create a holistic approach to living with greater awareness and resilience. Whether you are seeking to improve your self-knowledge, enhance your relationships, or simply live with a stronger sense of peace and security, this journey offers a powerful foundation for inner growth and connection. Through understanding your star sign, balancing your chakras, and strengthening your energetic boundaries, you open yourself to a life of greater harmony, compassion, and authentic love.

Aries (March 21 - April 19) – The Passionate Pioneer

As the first sign of the zodiac, Aries is known for its boldness, independence, and unyielding energy. Ruled by

Mars, the planet of action, Aries lovers are passionate and intense, often diving headfirst into relationships. They crave excitement and are drawn to partners who match their enthusiasm.

In relationships, Aries can be impulsive and direct. They express their feelings openly, often preferring honesty over sugar-coating. While this candor can bring clarity to relationships, it can also lead to conflicts if their partner prefers a softer approach. Aries partners thrive when they are given room to explore, grow, and lead. In turn, they bring a fresh, adventurous energy to relationships, making every day feel like an exciting new chapter.

Taurus (April 20 - May 20) – The Sensual Stalwart

Taurus, an earth sign ruled by Venus, is grounded, loyal, and highly sensual. Taureans approach love with caution, preferring stability over spontaneity. They value trust and loyalty above all else and will only commit when they feel truly secure with their partner.

In relationships, Taurus is devoted and dependable, often prioritizing their partner's needs and comfort. However, their strong need for stability can make them resistant to change, sometimes leading to a reluctance to compromise. A Taurus partner appreciates the finer things in life—romantic dinners, cozy evenings, and heartfelt gestures. They are most compatible with partners who value loyalty and are willing to invest time and energy in building a solid foundation.

Gemini (May 21 - June 20) – The Communicative Chameleon

Gemini, ruled by Mercury, is a curious, quick-witted, and adaptable sign. Known for their dual nature, Geminis bring versatility and intellectual stimulation to relationships. They love engaging conversations, shared interests, and mental stimulation, and they thrive with partners who can keep up with their ever-changing interests.

In relationships, Gemini can be unpredictable but incredibly charming. They are excellent communicators, often using words to express their feelings in a thoughtful way. However, their need for variety can sometimes make them restless. Gemini partners seek connection on both an intellectual and emotional level, and they are happiest with partners who can stimulate their minds as well as their hearts.

Cancer (June 21 - July 22) – The Nurturing Protector

Cancer is a deeply emotional, empathetic, and protective water sign ruled by the Moon. Cancers approach relationships with caution, often hiding their vulnerability until they feel completely safe. They are nurturing by nature, creating an atmosphere of love and care for their partners.

In relationships, Cancer is deeply committed and loyal. They go to great lengths to provide emotional support, often intuitively sensing their partner's needs. However, their sensitivity can lead them to take things personally, and they may withdraw if they feel hurt. Cancer partners are happiest with those who value emotional depth, trust, and security, making them an ideal match for partners who seek a lasting, stable connection.

Leo (July 23 - August 22) – The Charismatic Lover

Leo, ruled by the Sun, is a confident, warm-hearted, and magnetic fire sign. Known for their charisma and zest for life, Leos are passionate lovers who bring drama, romance, and excitement to relationships. They thrive when they are admired and appreciated.

In relationships, Leos are generous, loyal, and protective of their loved ones. However, they may crave attention and admiration, which can create challenges if their partner isn't naturally expressive. Leo partners are happiest with those who encourage their dreams, celebrate their successes, and offer plenty of love and attention in return. When a Leo feels cherished, they are one of the most devoted and loyal partners in the zodiac.

Virgo (August 23 - September 22) – The Thoughtful Companion

Virgo, an earth sign ruled by Mercury, is practical, analytical, and devoted. Known for their meticulous attention to detail, Virgos bring a thoughtful, grounded approach to relationships. They often show their love through acts of service and thoughtful gestures, valuing sincerity and honesty.

In relationships, Virgos are attentive and supportive, often going out of their way to make their partner feel loved. However, their perfectionist tendencies can lead to critical behavior if they feel things aren't "just right." Virgo partners are most compatible with those who appreciate their reliability and value the little things they do to make the relationship thrive.

Libra (September 23 - October 22) – The Harmonious Romantic

Libra, ruled by Venus, is a diplomatic, charming, and relationship-oriented air sign. Known for their love of beauty and harmony, Libras are natural romantics who seek balanced and harmonious relationships. They are drawn to beauty and often enjoy creating an aesthetically pleasing, peaceful environment for their partner.

In relationships, Libra is affectionate, fair, and considerate, often striving to meet their partner's needs. However, their tendency to avoid conflict can lead to unresolved issues if they are not careful. Libra partners are happiest with those who value open communication, shared values, and a deep connection.

Scorpio (October 23 - November 21) – The Intense Soulmate

Scorpio is a water sign ruled by Pluto, embodying intensity, passion, and mystery. Known for their deep emotions and intuitive nature, Scorpios approach relationships with a sense of all-or-nothing commitment. They crave depth, loyalty, and authenticity.

In relationships, Scorpios are loyal and fiercely protective of their loved ones. They can be possessive and may struggle with trust issues, but they give their whole heart to those they love. Scorpio partners seek a partner who values emotional connection and is willing to embrace the highs and lows of love.

Sagittarius (November 22 - December 21) – The Adventurous Partner

Sagittarius, ruled by Jupiter, is a fire sign known for its love of adventure, freedom, and optimism. Sagittarians approach love with an open heart, often seeking partners who share their zest for life and exploration. They thrive on new experiences and enjoy partners who value independence.

In relationships, Sagittarius is spontaneous and playful. They bring a sense of fun and adventure but may struggle with commitment if they feel confined. Sagittarius partners are happiest with those who support their need for independence and enjoy exploring new possibilities together.

Capricorn (December 22 - January 19) – The Loyal Partner

Capricorn, ruled by Saturn, is an earth sign characterized by ambition, loyalty, and practicality. Capricorns approach relationships with a strong sense of responsibility and often prioritize long-term commitment. They are drawn to partners who share their values and dedication.

In relationships, Capricorns are dependable and committed. They may seem reserved at first but open up as they build trust. Capricorn partners value consistency, loyalty, and shared goals, and they thrive with partners who are equally committed to building a future together.

Aquarius (January 20 - February 18) – The Independent Visionary

Aquarius, ruled by Uranus, is an air sign known for its intellectual curiosity, independence, and progressive outlook. Aquarians value individuality and often seek partners who support their quest for freedom and self-expression.

In relationships, Aquarius is loyal and caring but may struggle with overly emotional displays. They are most compatible with partners who value intellectual connection, freedom, and mutual respect. Aquarius partners are happiest with those who appreciate their unique perspective and share their vision for a better world.

Pisces (February 19 - March 20) – The Empathetic Dreamer

Pisces, ruled by Neptune, is a compassionate, intuitive, and imaginative water sign. Known for their empathy and sensitivity, Pisceans bring depth and creativity to relationships. They are dreamers who seek a partner who can connect with them on a soulful level.

In relationships, Pisces is gentle, romantic, and understanding. They may become overly absorbed in their partner's needs, sometimes at the expense of their own well-being. Pisces partners are happiest with those who respect their emotional needs and support their dreams.

Understanding the Zodiac Signs and Their Influence in Relationships, Enhanced by Chakra Insights

In astrology, each zodiac sign represents unique personality traits that influence not only how we perceive the world but also how we engage in relationships. The twelve zodiac signs provide a map of behavioral patterns, emotional responses, and compatibilities, which can help us understand ourselves and our partners. To deepen this exploration, we can look at how each sign aligns with the chakras—the seven energy centers in the body, according to ancient Eastern philosophies. When balanced, these chakras allow energy to flow smoothly, enhancing our emotional and relational well-being. By combining the insights of both the zodiac and chakras, we can cultivate a more harmonious and conscious approach to love and relationships.

Aries (March 21 - April 19) – The Passionate Pioneer, Root Chakra

As a sign ruled by Mars, Aries is all about taking action, embracing independence, and facing challenges head-on. Aries embodies the energy of the Root Chakra (Muladhara), which is located at the base of the spine and represents stability, security, and survival instincts. In relationships, Aries' strong Root Chakra energy gives them a solid sense of self and a drive to protect and support their partner. When balanced, Aries brings stability and energy; however, if this chakra is unbalanced, they may become possessive or overly aggressive.

In love, Aries needs a partner who appreciates their bold nature and encourages their independence. When they are grounded in their Root Chakra, they can offer a stable foundation to their partner while pursuing mutual growth.

Taurus (April 20 - May 20) – The Sensual Stalwart, Sacral Chakra

Taurus, ruled by Venus, aligns with the Sacral Chakra (Svadhisthana), located in the lower abdomen and associated with sensuality, creativity, and emotional depth. Taureans are deeply attuned to their senses and value loyalty, stability, and comfort. Their Sacral Chakra connection gives them a profound capacity for love, pleasure, and commitment. When balanced, Taurus can express their love through meaningful gestures, prioritizing their partner's well-being and creating a nurturing environment.

An imbalanced Sacral Chakra, however, may cause Taurus to become stubborn, possessive, or overly dependent on physical comforts. In relationships, Taurus thrives with partners who share their appreciation for loyalty and who are willing to invest emotionally.

Gemini (May 21 - June 20) – The Communicative Chameleon, Throat Chakra

Ruled by Mercury, Gemini is connected to the Throat Chakra (Vishuddha), which governs communication, expression, and understanding. Geminis are known for their lively conversation, wit, and ability to adapt to different social situations. With a strong Throat Chakra, they can articulate their feelings, engage in stimulating conversations, and express themselves authentically.

However, if this chakra is blocked or unbalanced, Gemini may struggle to communicate their emotions or may come across as indecisive. In relationships, Gemini needs a partner who values communication and is open to exploring new ideas, helping them to keep their Throat Chakra in alignment.

Cancer (June 21 - July 22) – The Nurturing Protector, Heart Chakra

Cancer, a water sign ruled by the Moon, resonates with the Heart Chakra (Anahata), located in the chest and associated with love, compassion, and empathy. Cancers are emotionally driven, nurturing, and highly protective of their loved ones. Their connection to the Heart Chakra allows them to offer unconditional love and create a warm, supportive environment for their partner.

When their Heart Chakra is balanced, Cancers are able to love freely and express their emotions openly. However, an unbalanced Heart Chakra may cause them to be overly sensitive, insecure, or clingy. In relationships, Cancer partners thrive when their emotional needs are met and reciprocated, and they seek a partner who values emotional intimacy and commitment.

Leo (July 23 - August 22) – The Charismatic Lover, Solar Plexus Chakra

Leo, ruled by the Sun, is connected to the Solar Plexus Chakra (Manipura), located just above the navel and associated with personal power, confidence, and self-expression. Known for their charisma and vitality, Leos radiate warmth and love. Their strong Solar Plexus energy gives them a sense of purpose and the ability to bring joy and energy into their relationships.

When balanced, Leos are confident and able to offer unconditional love, though if the Solar Plexus Chakra becomes overactive, they may demand excessive attention or validation. In relationships, Leo is best paired with someone who can recognize and celebrate their strengths while also sharing in their passions.

Virgo (August 23 - September 22) – The Thoughtful Companion, Third Eye Chakra

Ruled by Mercury, Virgo is associated with the Third Eye Chakra (Ajna), located in the center of the forehead, which represents intuition, insight, and mental clarity. Virgos are practical, analytical, and deeply thoughtful. With a strong Third Eye Chakra, they possess a natural ability to see details that others may miss, making them empathetic and reliable partners.

When the Third Eye Chakra is balanced, Virgos are able to perceive their partner's needs intuitively. If it becomes blocked, they may overthink, become self-critical, or overly analytical. In relationships, Virgo thrives with a partner who values honesty, mutual support, and thoughtful communication.

Libra (September 23 - October 22) – The Harmonious Romantic, Heart Chakra

Libra, ruled by Venus, is also connected to the Heart Chakra (Anahata), just like Cancer. Libras are naturally romantic and seek balance and harmony in their relationships. With a well-balanced Heart Chakra, they are able to see both sides of a situation and bring peace and understanding to their partnerships.

When the Heart Chakra is balanced, Libra brings affection, fairness, and emotional intelligence to their relationships. However, if unbalanced, they may avoid conflict at all costs, leading to repressed feelings. In relationships, Libra thrives with a partner who values emotional connection, communication, and mutual respect.

Scorpio (October 23 - November 21) – The Intense Soulmate, Sacral Chakra

Scorpio, ruled by Pluto, aligns deeply with the Sacral Chakra (Svadhisthana). Scorpios are intense, passionate, and emotionally deep, often seeking relationships that involve profound intimacy and trust. The Sacral Chakra connection enhances Scorpio's natural magnetism and allows them to connect on a deeply emotional and physical level. When balanced, Scorpio can be incredibly devoted and empathetic, though an overactive Sacral Chakra may cause possessiveness or jealousy. In relationships, Scorpio partners thrive with someone who values depth, loyalty, and a willingness to explore emotions together.

Sagittarius (November 22 - December 21) – The Adventurous Partner, Solar Plexus Chakra

Sagittarius, ruled by Jupiter, is connected to the Solar Plexus Chakra (Manipura), much like Leo. Sagittarians are known for their adventurous spirit, independence, and optimism. With a balanced Solar Plexus Chakra, they bring enthusiasm, joy, and a sense of freedom to their relationships.

However, if this chakra becomes unbalanced, they may struggle with commitment or become restless. In relationships, Sagittarius thrives with a partner who shares their love for exploration and is open to both personal and shared growth.

Capricorn (December 22 - January 19) – The Loyal Partner, Root Chakra

Capricorn, ruled by Saturn, is closely aligned with the Root Chakra (Muladhara). Capricorns are practical, ambitious, and deeply committed to building a strong foundation in both their career and personal life. With a strong Root Chakra, they bring stability, loyalty, and dedication to their relationships.

When balanced, Capricorn is dependable and hardworking. However, an unbalanced Root Chakra may lead them to become overly focused on material success or detached. Capricorns thrive in relationships where they feel supported in their ambitions and can build a future together with a committed partner.

Aquarius (January 20 - February 18) – The Independent Visionary, Third Eye Chakra

Aquarius, ruled by Uranus, aligns with the Third Eye Chakra (Ajna). Known for their progressive thinking and innovative spirit, Aquarians value intellectual connection and independence. Their connection to the Third Eye Chakra allows them to approach relationships with insight and creativity.

If their Third Eye Chakra is balanced, Aquarius can bring unique perspectives and loyalty to their relationship. When unbalanced, they may struggle with intimacy or appear emotionally distant. Aquarius partners thrive with those who respect their individuality and share in their vision for positive change.

Pisces (February 19 - March 20) – The Empathetic Dreamer, Crown Chakra

Pisces, ruled by Neptune, resonates with the Crown Chakra (Sahasrara), located at the top of the head, which represents spiritual connection, intuition, and higher understanding. Pisceans are compassionate, intuitive, and sensitive to the energies around them. Their Crown Chakra alignment gives them a natural ability to empathize and connect on a soul level.

With a balanced Crown Chakra, Pisces can bring deep spiritual and emotional connection to their relationships. However, an overactive Crown Chakra may cause them to become overly idealistic or detached from reality. Pisces partners are happiest with those who value emotional depth, compassion, and shared dreams.

The interplay between zodiac signs and chakras offers a rich tapestry for understanding relationship dynamics. By aligning our chakras and tuning into the natural qualities of our zodiac signs, we can bring harmony, balance, and insight to our relationships. Each zodiac sign and its associated chakra offers different gifts, guiding us toward greater empathy, awareness, and growth in love. Relationships are not only about compatibility; they are about mutual respect, understanding,

Opening to True Love Through Understanding and Chakra Alignment

Understanding the connection between zodiac signs and chakras offers a powerful way to deepen your connection with both yourself and your partner. By becoming aware of each other's core needs, strengths, and vulnerabilities, you gain insights that go beyond surface traits, helping you understand the motivations behind your partner's actions and emotional responses. Astrology and chakras together create a roadmap, guiding you to honor your partner's unique personality while building a bond that is both supportive and empowering.

Each zodiac sign has its own qualities and preferred ways of connecting, from Taurus's need for stability to Aquarius's desire for intellectual stimulation. By learning these differences, you can adjust your expectations, find areas of common ground, and communicate in a way that honors both your needs and those of your partner. For example, if you know your partner is a Cancer, aligning with their Heart Chakra can help you cultivate warmth and emotional closeness. If they are a Sagittarius, activating your Solar Plexus Chakra can help you bring a spirit of adventure and openness into the relationship.

But true connection and soulmate relationships also require an internal commitment to growth and openness. This is where chakra work becomes essential. Blocked or imbalanced chakras can lead to misunderstandings, fear of intimacy, or emotional detachment, creating barriers to experiencing true love. By cleansing and balancing your chakras, you open yourself up to love that is pure, supportive, and lasting.

Here are some practical steps for balancing your chakras and cultivating a relationship open to true love:

1. **Practice Chakra Meditation and Visualization**

Meditation and visualization are powerful tools for chakra cleansing. Find a quiet place to sit, close your eyes, and visualize each chakra, starting at the Root Chakra and moving upward to the Crown. Imagine a healing light filling each chakra, removing any negativity or blockages. For example, visualize a bright red light at the Root Chakra to increase your sense of security and grounding, which is essential in establishing trust in relationships.

2. **Use Affirmations for Each Chakra**

Affirmations can help reinforce positive energy and remove doubts that may block your chakras. For example, say "I am safe and secure" to balance your Root Chakra, or "I am open to love" to cleanse the Heart Chakra. Repeating these affirmations regularly helps instill a positive mindset, allowing you to release old fears or insecurities that may have limited your ability to connect authentically.

3. **Incorporate Yoga and Physical Movement**

Yoga is a gentle yet powerful way to align and balance your chakras. Specific yoga poses activate and heal different chakras. For example, Tree Pose is grounding and beneficial for the Root Chakra, while Camel Pose opens the Heart Chakra, increasing your capacity for love and empathy. Incorporating regular yoga into your routine can help you maintain an energetic balance, making you more open and receptive in relationships.

4. **Embrace Self-Reflection and Emotional Healing**

Chakra work often involves examining past hurts or patterns that may have created blockages. Take time to reflect on any fears, insecurities, or past relationship wounds. Journaling or speaking with a therapist can be beneficial for processing these feelings. By understanding and releasing emotional baggage, you allow your Heart Chakra to open fully, making space for true love.

5. **Set Intentions and Practice Gratitude**

Setting clear intentions for what you desire in a relationship and expressing gratitude helps keep your Crown Chakra open, bringing in higher awareness and alignment. By focusing on what you appreciate in yourself and your partner, you shift to a more open, loving state that invites mutual respect and compassion.

6. **Practice Loving-Kindness Meditation with Your Partner**

In this form of meditation, sit together with your partner, close your eyes, and visualize sending love and gratitude toward one another. This practice opens both the Heart and Crown Chakras, creating a deep energetic bond. By regularly sharing loving energy, you both cultivate empathy, compassion, and understanding, which are essential for building a soulmate connection.

Embracing True Love and Soulmate Connections

When you align with your chakras and embrace the insights offered by zodiac signs, you create an inner and outer harmony that attracts authentic love. You become more aware of your needs and those of your partner, allowing for deeper intimacy and mutual growth. By cleansing and balancing your chakras, you clear away old fears and open yourself to the beauty of true connection, preparing your heart and mind for a soulmate relationship.

A soulmate is not merely someone who shares similar traits or preferences but someone who resonates with your soul's energy. With open chakras and a balanced approach, you bring your whole self into the relationship, creating a connection based on honesty, compassion, and understanding. This journey of self-discovery and alignment helps you not only attract love but sustain it, allowing for a relationship that is both fulfilling and transformative.

As you continue to balance your chakras and align with your zodiac insights, you invite more love, harmony, and joy into your life, embracing a path toward the true, soul-deep connections you seek.

Chapter 7

Conclusion

The End

Congratulations! You've completed the journey and have becoming A Star Mastering- The Feminine Enigma succeeded with confidence and resilience—you now have the man you desire"wrapped around your finger"! Now, let's look back and celebrate all that you've learned and accomplished along the way:

- **You've balanced emotions with reason:** You didn't let emotions rule but used a smart, balanced approach.
- **You've stayed loyal to true friends:** Real friends are there through thick and thin, and you haven't lost sight of this.
- **You've found your voice:** You confidently express yourself, even when opinions differ.
- You've kept him on his toes: You didn't let him get too comfortable; the spark is alive and well.
- **You've honored your mood, but you're in control:** You know when to follow your heart and when to stay grounded.

- **You respect and love yourself:** Your self-worth is unshakeable—you aren't giving in to his whims but instead staying true to what matters to you.
- **You know your priorities:** You won't settle for last-minute plans or being an afterthought.
- **You've mastered patience:** Both your inner strength and outer glow reflect your self-care and resilience.
- **You're at peace with yourself:** Your happiness radiates, creating a sense of calm and strength in your life.
- **You know when to retreat:** You've learned to protect your private life and withdraw at the right time.
- **Your health is non-negotiable:** You're putting yourself first.
- **You're multi-dimensional and vibrant:** With a sense of adventure, confidence, and playfulness, you are many wonderful sides in one incredible woman.
- **You've stopped making excuses for him:** You're realistic about his flaws and refuse to deceive yourself.
- **You're not his bank:** Your support is emotional, not financial.
- **You are an investment in his life:** He values your presence, and you know your worth.
- **You embrace your bold spirit:** Your zest for life brings joy and excitement to every moment.

- **You understand him deeply:** You know his nature and handle his emotions while keeping the power in your hands. Your lighthearted jealousy and independence make you irresistible.

This book is meant to be your companion—revisit it when life gets tough, and remember the confidence, perspective, and strength you've gained. Every woman faces vulnerable times, but the smart ones rise with even more self-belief, clarity, and beauty.

We hope this book has empowered you to live the life you dream of, just like so many who've embraced these principles. There's much more to explore, but first, focus on "A Star Is Born" and let it sink in deeply. We've distilled these ideas for you, keeping them close to your heart and easy to grasp. Don't miss the message or the inspiration it carries.

Love yourself —and remember, you are always, always stronger than you think. As we reach the end of this journey together, pause for a moment to reflect on all that you've uncovered and achieved. When you first picked up this book, maybe you were feeling worn down, undervalued, or even invisible. Perhaps love and happiness seemed just out of reach, a constant chase that left you exhausted. But now, after taking this path, you've uncovered something remarkable: the power within you to reclaim control, to step into a life led by purpose, respect, and genuine self-worth.

You've transformed not just your view of relationships but your relationship with yourself.

Throughout these pages, you have gained tools, insights, and a newfound clarity. You've learned how to bring out your inner strength with confidence and grace, how to build boundaries rooted in self-respect, and how to cultivate resilience in a way that doesn't harden you but empowers you. You've discovered the liberating power of self-love—the kind that doesn't depend on anyone else's validation, that doesn't seek approval, but that quietly fuels you from within. And through this shift, you've seen how it inspires others to respond differently to you, to value and cherish you in a way you once might have only dreamed about.

But remember, the goal has never been simply about "winning" someone over or shaping yourself to fit anyone else's mold. This journey has always been about coming home to yourself—reclaiming your voice, your desires, and your innate worth. The kind of love you're seeking, the kind that endures and fulfills, begins with two individuals who are whole and confident in who they are, who choose each other without compromise or compromise of self.

As you move forward, think of this book as a guide, a reminder of the strength and wisdom that now belong to you. Let it serve as a testament to your journey back to yourself. You are the leading lady of your story, the woman who lives a life that excites and challenges her, who welcomes love that fulfills rather than depletes. You deserve a relationship that honors the fullness of who you are. You deserve to be cherished as an equal and valued as irreplaceable.

So take a deep breath and let the final words of this book settle within you. Hold your head high, let your heart remain open, and carry forward this wisdom with pride. Your journey isn't over—it has only just begun. Embrace each new chapter with the assurance that you are capable of building a life of joy, connection, and meaning. Keep pushing boundaries, keep honoring your worth, and keep living unapologetically, for you deserve nothing less.

And remember, love may come into your life and captivate your heart, but it is you who hold the key to your own happiness. Keep that key safe, and let it guide you as you step boldly into this new chapter.

The Eternal Dance of Souls

In the journey to understanding soulmates, we see how the idea of a destined connection transcends cultures, religions, and eras, illuminating a universal truth about love and companionship.

Embracing the Soulmate Connection

Whether seen as a covenant in Christianity, a divine partnership in Islam, a predestined bond in Judaism, or a spiritual journey in Buddhism, soulmates represent the deep connections that transform our lives. Recognizing and embracing this bond requires openness, resilience, and faith.

The Global Tapestry of Soulmates

Soulmates are celebrated worldwide, each culture and faith bringing unique perspectives to this connection. The diversity of these beliefs enriches our understanding, showing us that while love can take countless forms, its essence is shared.

Beyond Romance: The Many Faces of Soulmates

Soulmates are often seen as romantic partners, but this bond can extend to friends, mentors, or even family. These connections are crucial to our spiritual evolution, bringing people into our lives who challenge, uplift, and guide us.

The Spiritual Evolution of Soulmates
A soulmate relationship often accelerates personal and spiritual growth, pushing us toward deeper understanding and compassion. By embracing the soulmate journey, we can find purpose and clarity within ourselves.

Final Reflections: Embracing the Soulmate Journey

The journey of soulmates is an eternal dance, a blend of joy, growth, and reflection. To truly experience this connection, we must approach it with open hearts, ready to learn and evolve. For those who find a soulmate, whether in romantic love or through profound friendship, the journey is transformative.

The Soulmate Concept in LGBTQ+ Relationships

Soulmate connections know no boundaries, including gender or orientation. In LGBTQ+ relationships, the essence of a soulmate remains the same—a bond of deep understanding, mutual growth, and a shared sense of belonging.

Through this timeless journey, we come to understand that soulmates are not merely destined partners but profound reflections of our deepest selves. By honoring the diversity and depth of these relationships, we cultivate a richer, more inclusive view of love.

As we reach the end of this journey together, I want you to take a moment to reflect on all you've uncovered. You started this book seeking change, perhaps feeling worn down, undervalued, or even invisible. You may have felt like the love and happiness you craved were somehow always out of reach. But now, as you've worked through each chapter, you've learned that reclaiming control and stepping into your own power is not only possible—it's transformative.

By embracing these strategies and stepping into the role of a woman who commands respect and admiration, you've

begun to reshape not only your relationships but also your life. You've learned the art of emotional resilience, the thrill of subtle mystery, and the undeniable power of self-love. You've discovered that you don't need to chase validation or approval; you're capable of inspiring him to be the one who pursues you, cherishes you, and can't imagine his life without you. You are the woman who moves with purpose, who understands her worth, and who lets nothing and no one define her except herself.
But remember, this isn't just a transformation for the sake of "winning" a relationship. This journey has been about reclaiming yourself—your desires, your confidence, and your individuality. A truly healthy, balanced relationship begins with two whole individuals who choose each other without losing themselves. The man who deserves you is one who sees and honors all of your complexities, who treasures your confidence and respects your boundaries. By standing strong in your worth, you invite him to meet you there, to step up to the challenge, and to value you as an equal and as an irreplaceable partner.

As you move forward, let this book be a reminder: you are the leading lady of your own story. You deserve to live a life that excites you, a love that fulfills you, and a partnership that enhances every part of who you are. Don't let anyone or anything convince you otherwise.

So, take a deep breath and hold your head high. Embrace the wisdom you've gained and carry it forward with pride. The journey isn't over—it's only just begun. Keep pushing boundaries, keep honoring your worth, and keep living boldly and unapologetically.

Remember, he may be captivated by your presence, but you hold the key to your happiness.

"Love yourself first"